CROSSING by *faith*

Sermons on the Journey
from Youth to Adulthood

David L. Bartlett, Claudia A. Highbaugh,
and Stephen Butler Murray, editors

CHALICE
PRESS

ST. LOUIS, MISSOURI

Biblical quotations, unless otherwise noted, are from the *New Revised Standard Version Bible*, copyright 1989, Division of Christian Education of the National Council of the Churches of Christ in the United States of America. Used by permission. All rights reserved.

Scripture quotations marked NKJV are taken from the *New King James Version.* Copyright © 1979, 1980, 1982 by Thomas Nelson, Inc. Used by permission. All rights reserved.

Excerpt on page 140 from *On the Pulse of Morning* by Maya Angelou, copyright © 1993 by Maya Angelou. Used by permission of Random House, Inc.

Cover art: © Getty Images
Cover and interior design: Elizabeth Wright

This book is printed on acid-free, recycled paper.

Visit Chalice Press on the World Wide Web at
www.chalicepress.com

10 9 8 7 6 5 4 3 2 1   03 04 05 06 07 08

Library of Congress Cataloging–in–Publication Data

Crossing by faith : sermons on the journey from youth to adulthood / David L. Bartlett, Claudia A. Highbaugh, and Stephen Butler Murray, ed[itor]s.— 1st ed.
  p. cm.
Includes bibliographical references.
  ISBN 0-8272-0492-2 (alk. paper)
  1. Youth—Religious life—Sermons. 2. Sermons, American. I. Bartlett, David Lyon, 1941- II. Highbaugh, Claudia A. (Claudia Ann) III. Murray, Stephen Butler. IV. Title.
  BV4531.3.C76 2003
  252'.55—dc22

                                                     2003015354

Printed in the United States of America

Contents

Contributors

Carla Aday is minister of community development at Country Club Christian Church (Disciples of Christ) in Kansas City, Missouri.

Wesley D. Avram is Clement-Muehl Assistant Professor of Communication at Yale University Divinity School, New Haven, Connecticut.

David L. Bartlett is dean of academic affairs and Lantz Professor of Preaching and Christian Communication at Yale University Divinity School.

Alison L. Boden is dean of Rockefeller Memorial Chapel at the University of Chicago in Chicago, Illinois.

William Sloane Coffin is former senior pastor of The Riverside Church in New York City and former university chaplain and pastor of the Church of Christ at Yale University, New Haven, Connecticut.

Peter J. Gomes is Plummer Professor of Christian Morals and Pusey Minister in the Memorial Church at Harvard University, Cambridge, Massachusetts.

Claudia Ann Highbaugh is chaplain and lecturer on ministry at Harvard University Divinity School, Cambridge, Massachusetts.

Ruthanna B. Hooke is assistant professor of homiletics at Virginia Theological Seminary in Alexandria, Virginia.

Scott Black Johnston is associate professor of homiletics at Austin Presbyterian Theological Seminary, Austin, Texas.

Serene Jones is professor of theology at Yale University Divinity School, New Haven, Connecticut.

Peter Laarman is senior minister of Judson Memorial Church in New York City.

Barbara K. Lundblad is Joe R. Engle Associate Professor of Preaching at Union Theological Seminary, New York.

Wayne A. Meeks is Woolsey Professor Emeritus of Biblical Studies at Yale University, New Haven, Connecticut.

Stephen Butler Murray is College Chaplain, Associate Director of the Intercultural Center, and Lecturer in Philosophy and Religion at Skidmore College, Saratoga Springs, New York.

Richard E. Spalding is College Chaplain and Coordinator of Community Service at Williams College in Williamstown, Massachusetts.

Frederick J. Streets is University Chaplain and Pastor of the Church of Christ at Yale University, New Haven, Connecticut.

Richard F. Ward is Associate Professor of Preaching and Performance Studies at Iliff School of Theology, Denver, Colorado.

William H. Willimon is Dean of the Chapel and Professor of Christian Ministry at Duke University, Durham, North Carolina.

INTRODUCTION

On Harry Baker Adams

David L. Bartlett

In his 1995 Lyman Beecher Lectures, *Preaching: The Burden and the Joy*, Harry Baker Adams writes of the kind of preaching that has marked much of his own work:

> There are sermons intended for *formation*. There were occasions when Jesus addressed his listeners with the invitation, 'Come, follow me.' Some people left their work, their homes, their families, their communities to go after him…The sermon was not a call for an initial commitment to him. Rather, it was a sermon designed to help his followers grow in their understanding of what it meant to be faithful and in their capacity to be his followers.[1]

In his ministry as a teacher, administrator, university chaplain, and master of a residential college, Harry Adams has helped us think about Christian formation. Because of his location as a guide

---

[1]Harry Baker Adams, *Preaching: The Burden and the Joy* (St. Louis: Chalice Press, 1996), 121.

at the crossroads where people are making life decisions, he has been especially helpful in enabling people to move toward deeper commitment and truer discipleship. This collection of sermons and essays is an attempt to draw on themes that have been evident in Harry Adams's own ministry and preaching. How do we understand our identity and how can life's transitions be opportunities as well as challenges? How do we preach and counsel and guide in times of personal or social crisis? What are the marks of Christian hospitality, and what does Christian community look like when it is genuinely hospitable? How can we understand our jobs, indeed our lives, as vocations—standing under the call and the promise of God?

Reflecting on his own vocation as a minister to Yale students, especially undergraduates, Adams noted how often the issues of identity, transition, and vocation come together in the lives of students. College students need to be liberated from bondage to parental expectations. Part of claiming their adulthood is claiming distance from the goals and aspirations that their families project on them. College students (and other younger adults as well) need to be liberated from bondage to their own early impulsive commitments. Often Adams's pastoral response to a student who had early on announced that she intended to be a lawyer was to help her understand that an early ambition is not necessarily a lifetime commitment. Other younger people seek to avoid the notion of vocation entirely. College can prove so comfortable a setting that issues of what to do next simply never arise. The sensitive minister will need to nudge from time to time, to remind students that graduation is coming, and that graduation really is commencement: the beginning of new possibilities and responsibilities.

Related to these questions of transition, identity, and vocation, says Adams, are the questions of values, for many the questions of faith. How does one decide on a vocation when the pressures of society may insist that the major purpose of an occupation is to make money, or when the university may insist that the only life worth living requires a Ph.D.? One of Harry Adams's gifts has been to help people understand the deeper values and hopes that drive them, to own their braver and more faithful selves.

As a member of the university community, Harry Adams has lived and taught through the crises of the last half of the twentieth century. During his ministry as chaplain of Yale University the issue that most tested his ministry was the Persian Gulf War. As a preacher, Harry Adams honored a variety of perspectives while still making clear his own sense of what was appropriate national policy.

Because Adams is himself a veteran, he is able to speak of hopes for peace and the integrity of pacifism with a kind of authority that many of us lack. His pastoral leadership during the Gulf War crisis was indicative of the way in which he leads through many crises. He articulated the issues. He tried to help students discover their own faith, their own values around issues of war and peace, military service, and pacifism. He reminded us that the human situation, and perhaps especially the political situation, is inevitably ambiguous. The answers are never as clear as we might hope. For that reason he encouraged his congregation and his counselees to learn to honor the positions of those whose response to the war was very different from their own.

The issue of identity and the challenge of conflict came together during Adams's ministry at Yale around the issue of sexuality. While always clear on his own values and standards, Adams encouraged students to understand the range of commitments and attachments that mark human sexuality. In particular he tried to make the university chapel and the colleges where he served places that were hospitable to people of different sexual orientations. At the same time he worked to make sure that those whose religious or ethical convictions made it difficult for them to accept other forms of sexuality, especially homosexuality, were also welcome in the communities where he served. Dissent was encouraged, not stifled.

As chaplain to the whole university, Adams balanced his own commitments as a minister of the Disciples of Christ community with his commitments to the diversity of the larger university. The chaplaincy provided a safe context for people to explore religious issues without feeling they would be subject to the pressures of proselytizing.

Chaplain Adams also sought to model hospitality to those whose religious commitments were different from his own. When Jewish students at Trumbull College were unable to use the electronic key card to get into their own college on the Sabbath because that violated strictures against particular kinds of work, Adams got them access to a back gate that could be opened with the perfectly acceptable old-fashioned key.

Similarly, as a teacher and administrator at Yale Divinity School, Harry Adams spent his career both helping students understand the gifts of their own denominations and traditions and helping them learn the challenge and opportunity that come from living and studying in a genuinely ecumenical setting.

Reflecting on how his mind has changed through his years of ministry, Adams commented on these same issues of conflict, diversity, and hospitality.

As with many others, his mind has changed on the place of homosexual people in society and in our churches. As pastor of a Welcoming and Affirming congregation, The Church of Christ at Yale, he and his wife Manette modeled both welcome and affirmation.

As he recalls his ministry as a member of a denomination especially committed to ecumenism, Harry Adams suggests that he has grown in his appreciation of the diversity of Christian denominational life. Now denominationalism seems not so much a problem as an opportunity—a way in which different communities can be faithful in different ways to the same Lord.

Summing up both his commitment to Christian faith and his openness to others, Harry Adams says that he has come to understand that people are often right in what they affirm, and often less right in what they deny. Christians have appropriately used the first part of John 14:6 to indicate their loyalty to Jesus: "I am the way, and the truth, and the life." Less appropriately, Christians have used the second half of that same verse as a way of condemning those who do not understand God's approach to humankind in the same way: "No one comes to the Father except through me."

Perhaps, Harry Adams suggests, if we discover the richness of our diverse affirmations, and are more reticent about the harshness of our denials, we will find ways to live more fully in human community, the kind of community he has encouraged and inspired for the years of his ministry.

Identity

1

Transitions in Who We Are

Stephen Butler Murray

When we are young and if we are lucky enough to be raised by good parents, they watch over and care for us in specific ways. They make sure that we are fed, that we are clothed, that we have a safe home in which to live, that our talents and abilities are nurtured, that we feel cherished and wanted. As we grow older and leave the canopy of their aegis, our parents gradually lose the ability to foster us in a protected space where we feel valued. This process begins when we go to school, where we are exposed to other children of varied backgrounds, to teachers with new ideas that can be threatening, to cultural shifts that may seem not only unfamiliar, but hostile to the very ways that our parents have viewed the world. We spend our adolescence on the periphery between these two states of being, the boundary that separates the familiarity of home and our tantalizingly innocent naïveté concerning the wider world. And oftentimes the new experiences we find outside of our homes may be not only appealing but also surprisingly consistent with a new vision of ourselves.

It is in this way that we begin to loose ourselves from the characteristics that were instilled by our upbringing, asserting instead new traits, different modes of being in the world. These are the components of a more mature identity, one whereby we have agency in determining who we are, how we shall be, what we claim as our own. This is not to say that the wider world does not influence us, for both beauty and tragedy permeate our lives, shaping and changing us in unforeseen ways. While we may never be the absolute architects of our own identity, we nonetheless discover a certain array of priorities that matter genuinely to us. These are commitments that stand resolute within us even though the world may be less constant, more unpalatable, than we would prefer. It is by these prerogatives that we navigate our way through the vagaries of life.

One way of reflecting on the formation of these prerogatives is through the process of naming. Think upon the story of Jacob wrestling with the angel at Peniel, when Jacob will not release the angel until it offers him a blessing. Think upon the story of Abram, who in making a covenant with God is renamed Abraham. Think upon Israel, whose very existence in the Hebrew scriptures as a nation, as a people, is based on the ongoing promises made between them and their God, an ongoing promise made by and for each new generation. So often in the Old Testament, the blessing is bestowed as a name, as an identity, as a way of being and living in the world.

It is important to realize that to be blessed is to be invested with more than a responsibility, but with a vocation toward living a good life. This good life is not necessarily the luxurious life, the existence in which we make our way with ease. The good life is not measured by the length of our days, but by the quality of those days. The good life is not defined necessarily by accomplishment, but by fulfillment. The good life may not be the life of appearing the best, but the life of being one's best.

I believe that when we are at our best, we try to live our life as though it were a prayer. As we grow older, we expand our prayers from those we offer at our bedside as children, to prayers that we offer in the pews of church, to prayers that we offer during times of crisis, to prayers that we offer in every lived moment of our lives. In this way, our better natures might infuse who we are throughout our lives, publicly, rather than be confined to our moments of deep meditation and careful consideration.

In essence, faith, when it truly is faith, is not meant to be something that we keep hidden in ourselves, for ourselves alone. Faith is not the lighthouse that illuminates our own darkness; faith is not the personal stash of food we horde for our own time of famine; and faith is not the inspiration we use merely as our own, private muse. Instead, faith flowers. Faith grows beyond its initial seed, beyond its first stalk, and it becomes more beautiful, more lovely, more powerful, more deep, until faith reaches a point that it blooms beyond itself. The fruits of our faith are exhibited in who we are, how we are in communication and in communion with one another, in community.

The theologian Paul Tillich once wrote that a person becomes a person in the encounter with persons and in no other way.[1] I agree, especially as that quote deals with matters of faith. And I say that because we become persons of faith only in the encounter with people of faith and in no other way. Left to our own devices, we make religion what we would make of it. Religion can become directionless, such that we begin to pray to a divine being of our own invention rather than to a God who created us, who loves us, and who hopes for us. On our own, religion and faith separate, become incoherent, and ultimately ineffectual. It is only when we explore our faith in the company of others, who also are on that life quest of discovering and navigating their own faith, that the seeds of faith, properly planted, bear the fruits that they promised would be their yield. Faith practiced alone is a folly, the very antithesis of loving our neighbor as ourselves. To share, to offer freely, to be vulnerable in one's faith: *that* is the rich, deep soil in which our faith might flourish.

We are called to accept one another, to serve one another, to accept the cost and joy of discipleship. My friend Alison Boden, Dean of Rockefeller Chapel at the University of Chicago, once wrote that "the moral test of spirituality is justice. I challenge students with that. The primary test for religion is not about feeling good about yourself. It's about being good, which means doing good."[2]

As we contemplate how it is that we come to our identity, it is important to remember that while others name us, we have a hand

---

[1]Paul Tillich, *Love, Power, and Justice: Ontological Analyses and Ethical Applications* (New York: Oxford Univ. Press, 1954), 78.

[2]Alison Boden, "Charity and Justice," *Criterion* 34 (1995): 13.

in deciding whether we will accept the names that are given to us. To make it concrete, to become part of a group is to take on the name of that group. For instance, to be a member of a church is to take on an identity that has certain social assumptions cast with it. To be named in community is to take on a shared mantle, and even sometimes a shared yoke. To be named is a blessing and a responsibility. Oftentimes, we focus only on one element, either the burden or the joy, but not both in mutuality. Life is not so simple as to be merely bad or merely good, though we have a tendency to trick ourselves that this is the case for a given time. Part of the experience of being human in this world is to bear both the wreaths of flowers and the weighty loads. Part of being a church is to celebrate together in community *and* to support one another during harsh times. Part of being a beloved child of God is to be confident that God cares for us *and* to despair that God can seem so very absent. All this comes with being named. But if we have no name, if we refuse to take one on, then we are not known, absent, adrift. To be named is to have a purpose, to have a world, to have a home.

It seems to me that what we want out of religion, quite often, is a sense of protection. We want to know that in all times and all places, God is with us. And we want to know that there is a real significance to that. What haunts us in the midst of uncertainty is that God's presence in our lives might merely be empty rhetoric. What frightens us is that at the end of the day, we shall be shattered by the realization that the very God to whom we have prayed and in whom we have placed our trust is as ephemeral as air. And that concern can be overwhelming in these times, debilitating our capacities to love and trust, move and breathe freely. If God might not be there, why invest ourselves in our faith? Why make faith integral to our identity?

In asking those questions, we confront a crossroads and come face to face with a choice. And more often than not, how we navigate that treacherous terrain is dependent on how we see ourselves in the world, how we understand the very basis of our identity. If we look upon ourselves and see flesh and bone that ultimately must encounter the world alone through our own skill, savvy, determination, and will, I believe that in the end we shall fail. In that case, life and loss can overcome us, because we can be depleted of our best resources, abandoned by the personal virtues on which we always relied. This is the sin of utter self-reliance. It is the belief that we, on the sufficiency of our initiative and drives, can survive anything. And it is just not true. More than anything else, our self-reliance can betray us and leave us famished.

The other alternative at the crossroads is to behold ourselves as needing something more than what we can provide on our own. It is to have the courage to admit that we are vulnerable, that we enjoy a certain necessity for others. And so we might be so bold, in our weakest moments, as to let others into our hearts, our homes, our very lives. That requires trust and it means that we risk the potential for being hurt even more than we already are. But it is also the occasion for hope, for seeing our future possibilities as something desirable and worth holding on to. To be hospitable is to invite others to do more than know who we are, but to shape, change, transform us. Through their influence, we bloom into someone beyond whom we are now or ever could become were we left to our own devices.

The very essence of our identity is not our individuality, but our communality. As self-determined as we are, the encounters we have with others, the experiences that comprise the moments of our lives, all join together to determine something of who we are as individuals living in communities that are themselves part of a greater network of societies. And indeed, for those who find themselves seekers and believers in something greater than themselves, the identity that endeavors to embrace us ultimately is not a name that we give ourselves, but the name by which God endows us as God's beloved children.

2

"May I?"

Richard F. Ward

This was the final sermon that Professor Ward preached in Marquand Chapel at Yale Divinity School as Yale's Clement-Muehl Associate Professor of Homiletics before taking a new position at the Iliff School of Theology in Denver, Colorado. It was a service of Word and Sacrament.

> The word that Isaiah son of Amoz saw concerning
>   Judah and Jerusalem.
> In days to come
> the mountain of the LORD's house
> shall be established as the highest of the mountains,
> and shall be raised above the hills;
> all the nations shall stream to it.
> Many peoples shall come and say,
> "Come, let us go up to the mountain of the LORD,
> to the house of the God of Jacob;
> that he may teach us his ways
> and that we may walk in his paths."

For out of Zion shall go forth instruction
and the word of the LORD from Jerusalem.
He shall judge between the nations,
and shall arbitrate for many peoples;
they shall beat their swords into plowshares,
and their spears into pruning hooks;
nation shall not lift up sword against nation,
neither shall they learn war any more.
O house of Jacob,
come let us walk
in the light of the LORD! (Isa. 2:1–5; cf. Mic. 2:1–4)

Once upon a time, in the country of your childhood, on a sidewalk in the neighborhood where you grew up, you stood in a line with some of your friends, ready to play your favorite game. One of your friends was taking her turn at leading you in it. She would call out your name! Then, "Take one giant step!" "Mother, may I?" you'd say. "Yes, you may!" And so you would. You'd stretch those little legs and cover as much ground as you could! On and on it would go like that. Giant steps and baby steps, middle-sized steps and even bunny hop steps, thrilled with "Yes, you may!" and frustrated with "No, you may NOT!" until you somehow got to where the leader was and took your turn at giving the commands and controlling the game.

The day was ending. You'd be out of school for Christmas break, so you could stay out a little later. The sun would be sinking behind the rooftops and filling the sky with a dark red afterglow. There would be a chill in the air as night started to fall. Lights that were hung for Christmas started to come on and the game would go on—even in the gathering cold and darkness. You weren't sure if there was time left to continue playing! Still you would line up and wait to hear your name called either by the leader, calling out instructions to you, or by your parent, calling you away.

If you let it do its work in your memory (and in your heart), Advent will turn a light on a moment like this one. A moment fully lived in time but nearly forgotten. A moment fully lived in expectation. Which voices would I hear as darkness gathered? A voice that would call me to continue the game with a giant leap or two or by putting one foot in front of the other? Or would I hear a voice that would call me out of the game altogether?

If we let Advent do its work on us, it will also turn a light on the moment you and I are sharing right now. As the darkness gathers at the end of this year, I know that I am being called away from Yale Divinity School. I know that I am being called to a new place—with the new year will come new responsibilities for me and an uncertain future for me and for my family.

It is hard to leave this game.

I was given permission to take some giant steps here. Here I also found the strength to simply put one foot in front of another and make it through. Here I was able to take a turn at standing in front and calling out instructions to some of the best people I will ever know. Here I received direction and counsel and encouragement.

I am leaving. You are staying. Darkness is gathering. The game we have been in will go on. An uncertain future is breaking, for me and for you.

If we let Advent do its work on us, we will catch a glimpse of the future that God has in mind. These texts show us that the small remembered moments and the present one we are fully experiencing now are parts of a much bigger drama unfolding within the loving providence of God.

Although you and I will now be taking different paths, we are moving slowly, steadily to a place where God will consummate creation. Sometimes that happens in great leaps. Sometimes it is all we can do to put one foot in front of another. However we are getting there, and by whatever path we are headed to a place—in time—hidden in the mind and heart of God—where God will be fully recognized. We wait for a time when all nations will learn God's ways, a time when God will act to establish peace and justice on earth for all of humanity.

When God entered the game with us as Jesus, even we Gentiles received instruction in the rules, even we Gentiles became disciples. When Jesus was called out of the game through his death and resurrection, God turned the light on to a new community. A community that included us. We who were Not-a-People, in Hosea's words (Hos. 1:0–10), joined the house of Jacob and began walking in the light of the Lord!

Even though we have been walking in that light for two thousand years, we Christians have trouble believing the word God entrusted to the prophets of Israel and the apostles. "The war between God and all humankind is over!" they declare. God does not want to bring creation to a cataclysmic end!

In fact, God wants to make peace between the nations! God wants to teach them how to live in peace and learn to make war no more! Stop playing guessing games about God's timetable! Stop trying to write the script for God to follow! Instead lift up those places in your own minds and hearts and in your own communities of faith where you will recognize and worship the one true God and recite the instruction God will freely give! With the freedom that God gives, we still choose to make swords instead of plowshares. We still choose to live in conflict and hostility with our neighbors. We'd still rather exchange tinsel and trinkets instead of signs of lasting peace.

Still, God has not deserted us. God knows that light doesn't come at Advent only to expose the gap between God and God's people. Lights start to come on to show us that God has not left us to play our life games in the darkness against an empty sky. God does not call us out of the structures of our lives in order to leave us stranded and alone. God does not open doors we have closed in our communities of faith in order to bring in those who would destroy it, but those who would help to build it. It is God's dream to make a new humanity. And if we are to share in that dream, we may have to move from where we are now, to where God is calling us to be.

Here is the promise. When God does call our name, and we dare to heed that call over the din of the holiday season, the new steps we take will be toward the light of God. We will be moving toward that moment envisioned by Micah: "they shall all sit under their own vines and under their own fig trees, and no one shall make them afraid" (Mic. 4:4).

Let us then move, you and I, in the direction of God's voice. Let us move to this table God has prepared. Let us walk in the light of our God.

"Christian! Take one small step!" God, may I?

"Yes, you may."

3

"Bad Shepherds and Good"

Scott Black Johnston

I am the good shepherd. The good shepherd lays down his life for the sheep. The hired hand, who is not the shepherd and does not own the sheep, sees the wolf coming and leaves the sheep and runs away—and the wolf snatches them and scatters them. The hired hand runs away because a hired hand does not care for the sheep. I am the good shepherd. I know my own and my own know me, just as the Father knows me and I know the Father. And I lay down my life for the sheep. I have other sheep that do not belong to this fold. I must bring them also, and they will listen to my voice. So there will be one flock, one shepherd. For this reason the Father loves me, because I lay down my life in order to take it up again. No one takes it from me, but I lay it down of my own accord. I have power to lay it down, and I have power to take it up again. I have received this command from my Father. (Jn. 10:11–18)

16

The first Bible verse I memorized for Sunday school was the initial verse of the Twenty-third Psalm: "The Lord is my shepherd, I shall not want." My reward for having committed this simple passage to heart was a white plastic glow-in-the-dark figure—a robed Jesus holding a shepherd's crook and a rescued sheep. I placed it on my dresser, right under the lamp that sat there, so that it could "charge" in the light. Each evening, after my prayers were finished, covers tucked, and kisses administered, one of my parents turned out the light. Yet, of course, it was not completely dark in my room. My plastic Jesus was there emitting a yellow-green glow, and casting eerie shadows on a six year-old's wall. I found it comforting, mostly. "The Lord is my shepherd."

In the tenth chapter of John's gospel, Jesus adopts the rustic imagery of the Twenty-third Psalm in referring to himself, when he states, "I am the good shepherd." Like my plastic, iridescent Jesus, I find this declaration to be comforting, but not entirely. Allow me to explain. Generally speaking, having a shepherd is supposed to be a soothing notion. Shepherds care for sheep. Shepherds seek out pastures where there is lush grass and clear water for their flock. And, as my plastic Jesus shows, shepherds would go to great ends to rescue their wooly charges from precarious situations. All in all, having a metaphorical shepherd sounds like quite a blessing. Yet, if having a shepherd is so clearly to our advantage, why then does Jesus tell us that he is the "good" shepherd? Echoing the message of the psalm, he could have simply said, "I am your shepherd." Instead, Jesus implies a contrast. He hints that circumstances might be different. "I am the *good* shepherd." Hmm, meaning what, Jesus? Meaning that there are "bad" shepherds?

The possibility of "bad" shepherds hooked my curiosity, so I began hunting around—looking for bad shepherds. The search did not take very long. It turns out that the scripture is actually replete with shepherds who have been anything but good. In the book of Jeremiah, God calls the rulers of Judah "stupid" shepherds, poor leaders who have allowed their flocks to become scattered (Jer. 10:21). In the book of Ezekiel, God describes the leaders of the people as wicked shepherds. These shepherds do not feed the sheep, they slay the sheep and eat them. They do not care for the sheep; they ignore their flock's diseases and do not bind up their injuries. They do not love the sheep; they rule over them with harshness and violence (Ezek. 34: 1–11). Bad shepherds, indeed.

It turns out that when Jesus starts talking about shepherds and sheep, we cannot assume that the images that pop into listeners' minds are all warm and cuddly, gentle farmers frolicking on green hillsides with their fuzzy lambs. Mention shepherds in ancient Palestine, and people would likely recall all of the bad shepherds in their history, and the way in which people suffered in their custody. Most of us have known bad shepherds too—people with responsibility for leadership, for nurture, for teaching, for building up community; yet somewhere along the line, these folks stopped caring about their flock. They got so caught up in politics, so focused on making a name for themselves, so concerned with the size of their paycheck that they sold out. They became bad shepherds, and their sheep suffered because of it.

In the movie *Erin Brockovich*, Julia Roberts plays a legal assistant who discovers that a power plant belonging to a particularly large energy company in California has poisoned the surrounding groundwater with toxic selenium. To cover up, the company disguises its involvement, lies to its own workers, and pressures the local citizens to ignore the facts. In an instant, any obligation toward its employees and any degree of care that the business had for its host community was abandoned. Bad shepherds can turn on you pretty quickly. As Jesus says, when the wolf comes, the hired hand runs away. In fact, there could not be a worse predicament for the sheep: a bad shepherd on one side, and the wolf on the other. Given the many "evil" shepherds out there, it ought to comfort us that Jesus refers to himself as the "good" shepherd.

But, what (really) is a "good" shepherd? Such a person may be difficult to describe, both for the people of Israel and for us, because experience has filled our albums with more pictures of bad shepherds than good. Fortunately, Jesus does give content to the claim that he is the "good" shepherd. Listen to his description of a good shepherd. The good shepherd knows his sheep very well. The good shepherd is connected to the flock in a way that the hired hand is not. Hence, the good shepherd lays down his life for the sheep. The good shepherd sacrifices all for those in his care. Wait a minute. The good shepherd "lays down his life for the sheep"? Five times in this brief passage from John's gospel Jesus speaks of laying his life down. Why does he do this? Maybe we are to recall a figure from the Old Testament—young David (destined to be king), who as a shepherd boy risked his life slinging stones at lions and bears in order to protect his flock from voracious predators. Maybe Jesus is like David—a shepherd who will fight for us, and not run! Maybe. But I have to confess that this is precisely the point when I begin to worry.

Just how comforting is this passage? On a closer look, we may discover that we have assumed things that are not really in this text. For example, Jesus does *not* speak of battling the wolf when it comes. He simply says that the "good" shepherd lays down his life. Hmm, I wonder, what happens to the sheep when the shepherd is dead? If a leader sacrifices all, what good can he or she do for those left behind? Let me put it another way. If I were a Hollywood director filming the blockbuster movie *John 10,* I would cast tough-guy actor Bruce Willis as the "good" shepherd, Bruce Willis of the appropriately named *"Die Hard"* movies. When the wolf comes (played by John Malkovich, or maybe Christopher Walken) the other weak, bad, fearful shepherds would flee, leaving Bruce and the vulnerable sheep. A battle between the shepherd and the wolf would ensue. It would be a tense struggle, full of cliff-hanger moments, so that in many situations, the shepherd would actually be risking his life. But in the end, just as things look pretty bleak for the flock, the shepherd would triumph over the wolf. The sheep would cheer (or do whatever it is that sheep do to show extreme happiness and relief), and the credits would roll.

Speaking as a "sheep," I feel more secure with this version of the story. As a "sheep," I am willing to let the shepherd put his life at risk, but in the end, if anyone has to lay down his or her life, it had better be the wolf. Hopefully, some of you now see why I find this text to be less than completely comforting. The "good" shepherd that Jesus promises is not the kind of "good" that I want when predators come knocking.

A woman in a church where I recently preached came up to me and asked, "What's the deal with God?" She was angry. A few months earlier, her mother had died after a nasty struggle with cancer. For her family, the wolf came on a cold day in December. At the hospital bedside, this woman and her father heard the beast howling, and they prayed and prayed that the shepherd would drive it away; but despite their fervent intercessions, a beloved mother and wife was snatched away. "What's the deal with God?"

she asked. Many of us want to know what God is "up to" when the wolves circle the faithful sheep. Most of us wish that the "good" shepherd was a bit tougher, or at least more effective in protecting the flock. Yet, even as we plead for an "effective" shepherd, Christ presents us with a vulnerable one. Prompting a tricky, follow-up question, "What's so *good* about a vulnerable shepherd?" Or to raise the ante, in the words of theologian Bill Placher, "Of what use is a vulnerable God?"[1]

I know that none of you need homework to tell you that being vulnerable is a risky thing, a dangerous thing. Being "vulnerable" is usually not high on the list of characteristics we hope to embody. We want to be smart, and popular, and strong, and funny, but we are wary (appropriately so) of being vulnerable. For vulnerable people often end up being hurt people. And if we don't want to expose ourselves to injury, we really do not want to lay God open to being vulnerable. If you ask people, myself included, to describe God, most would say something about power. Many would say something about absolute power! That's what God is—a being with absolute power. I am not sure that this is wrongheaded. But we also want to know, "What's the deal with God's power?"

For the ancient Greeks, part of what it meant to have the power of a god was that deities were invulnerable. Some three hundred years before Christ, the Greek playwright Aristophanes dramatized this notion in his comedy *The Frogs*. In the course of this play two characters, Dionysius, the god, and Xanthias, the slave, travel through the underworld. The comedic tension in the drama lies in that both Dionysius and Xanthias claim to be gods. An argument ensues. Now to determine who really is a god and who is not (you would think that the distinction would be obvious), these two traveling companions devise an empirical test. Both will be flogged and, Xanthias proposes, "whichever of us squeals first or even bats an eyelid isn't a god at all."[2] The point is pretty clear: one of the perks of being a god is freedom from pain and suffering.

This is where the "good" shepherd messes up. For in laying his life down for the flock, Jesus disturbs the prevailing notion of how a god is supposed to behave. Clearly this is not Zeus, who

---

[1]William C. Placher, *Narratives of a Vulnerable God: Christ, Theology, and Scripture* (Louisville: Westminster John Knox Press, 1994), 4.

[2]Aristophanes, *The Frogs,* trans. David Barrett (London: Penguin Books, 1964), 179.

would drive the wolf away with thunderbolts. This is the Christ, who submits to the love of God and lays down his life. Over time, some Christians have tried to make the Christian God more invulnerable and Zeus-like by asserting that what suffered and died on the cross almost two thousand years ago was the "human part" of Jesus. Some even argue that the "divine part" of Jesus slipped out before the final events of the passion and Christ began to suffer. While such speculation *might* allow us to preserve our notions of an invulnerable God, most of Christian tradition has balked at that interpretation, leaving us in the uncomfortable position of confessing every Sunday that on that cross God too suffered and died. God suffers? God's life is laid down? What could that mean?

Jesus tells us that the "good" shepherd *knows* his sheep. How well do you think he knows those sheep? Does he know them like the hired hand knows them? Seeing them as a commodity to be raised, traded, moved around? This is, of course, an entirely sensible way to think about sheep.

When I was learning how to drive, my father took me out on some back roads in our rural Minnesota county—long stretches of graded gravel where the occasional tractor served as oncoming traffic. At one point in my lessons, I braked, and probably swerved too violently, on seeing a white-tailed deer standing by the side of the road. After we stopped, my gentle father praised my concern for the deer. He also cautioned me. "If there comes a point where swerving to miss an animal would place your own life in danger, then son," he said, "you hit the animal." It was good advice. It also reminds us how the hired hand thinks. When danger comes, the hired hand "knows" that his life is worth more than an animal's life, so he retreats to tend sheep another day.

How well does our God, the Holy One who is our shepherd, know the sheep? Does God also know them as a calculated risk? Or does God "know" in a much more intimate manner? "I know my own," says Jesus. And he does. He knows not from afar, but from up close—very close. In fact, he knows from experience not only what it is like to lose a sheep but also exactly what it is like to be snatched by the wolf.

Strangely enough, this is our Christian hope; that the Word did become flesh, that God risked becoming vulnerable like us, for us. This is the gift of the "good" shepherd—*a caretaker who knows exactly what it is like to be a sheep*. Now some of us, certainly me on most days, may pine for a God who throws thunderbolts at cancer and AIDS, who quickly removes despotic leaders, and who vanquishes depression before it even arrives. There are days when it seems like God could be doing a better job; but at those times, it may help to remember that "caring for" and "loving" creation were not very high on the list of "things to do today" for the invulnerable gods of yore. Then, perhaps, we can offer thanks that instead of a bigger, better, bullet-proof deity, Jesus presents us with a "good" one—a vulnerable, shepherd God. A God who *does* shed tears at whips, a God who *is* moved by human loss, a God who does not abandon us to the travails of life, but who suffers them with us, and consequently, a God who alone has the power to raise us up again, bringing life abundant. That's our God. A yellow-green light steadily glowing in the darkness. Our mostly comforting and so wholly "good" shepherd.

Amen.

4

"God in the Gaps"

Wesley D. Avram

This sermon was preached at the First Presbyterian Church of Wilmette, Illinois, on Easter Sunday, 1997.

When the sabbath was over, Mary Magdalene, and Mary the mother of James, and Salome bought spices, so that they might go and anoint him. And very early on the first day of the week, when the sun had risen, they went to the tomb. They had been saying to one another, "Who will roll away the stone for us from the entrance to the tomb?" When they looked up, they saw that the stone, which was very large, had already been rolled back. As they entered the tomb, they saw a young man, dressed in a white robe, sitting on the right side; and they were alarmed. But he said to them, "Do not be alarmed; you are looking for Jesus of Nazareth, who was crucified. He has been raised; he is not here. Look, there is the place they laid him. But go, tell his disciples and Peter that he is going ahead of you to

Galilee; there you will see him, just as he told you." So they went out and fled from the tomb, for terror and amazement had seized them; and they said nothing to anyone, for they were afraid. (Mk. 16:1–8)

Then Peter began to speak to them: "I truly understand that God shows no partiality, but in every nation anyone who fears him and does what is right is acceptable to him. You know the message he sent to the people of Israel, preaching peace by Jesus Christ—he is Lord of all. That message spread throughout Judea, beginning in Galilee after the baptism that John announced: how God anointed Jesus of Nazareth with the Holy Spirit and with power; how he went about doing good and healing all who were oppressed by the devil, for God was with him. We are witnesses to all that he did both in Judea and in Jerusalem. They put him to death by hanging him on a tree; but God raised him on the third day and allowed him to appear, not to all the people but to us who were chosen by God as witnesses, and who ate and drank with him after he rose from the dead. He commanded us to preach to the people and to testify that he is the one ordained by God as judge of the living and the dead. All the prophets testify about him that everyone who believes in him receives forgiveness of sins through his name." (Acts 10:34–43)

Have you ever died?

Have you ever breathed that odd sigh of relief that comes when you realize that you've been fighting for the wrong things, or spied through that crack in the facade of what sometimes passes for life and put your finger into that little space of light, pushing with the slightest effort in order to see through to another way of living?

She began to unwind her story during a long car ride to pick up a tardy participant in a spring retreat. We'd never talked before, but there's something about those times between leaving and arriving that tend to allow personal conversations:

"It happened during my first year at college," she told me. "My heart began to race while running on the playing field during a practice one afternoon. They pulled me off, and checked my blood pressure. It was through the roof. I was rushed to the hospital, and within ten minutes a doctor said to me, quite matter of fact, 'Don't run, don't walk more than a few steps, don't take any stairs. We'd prefer it if you'd just stay in bed. We're going to schedule you for open chest surgery next week to repair what we think is a congenital heart and circulation problem. This should have killed you before you ever entered your teens. Hadn't someone found this before? How in the world you've been an athlete all these years, we have no idea!'"

"Can you imagine?" she asked. "A college freshman. How was I supposed to feel?"

We talked about the surgery for a bit. Then she got more philosophical.

"As I think back on it now, I see that moment as the turning point of my life. I certainly fought it pretty hard for the first couple of years after it happened and I've drifted back and forth a bit since then, but I've come to believe that a change in me began that week, and has became permanent. Something arrived that will never let me go. I'm still on a quest to understand it, and live it, but the quest isn't for something I don't have. It's part of a desire to live well with what I *now* know."

"And what do you *now* know?" I asked.

"I know that it's all finished. It's really over. It's kind of perfect, in a way. You see…I've died. There's no going back. Every day is new. It's like someone took my life away from me, and a miracle gave it back. And I just can't believe that people don't get it. They're so foolish, like they've been invited to this massive feast and have purposely decided to go hungry instead. I guess they haven't died yet. They don't know that all the running and chasing and fretting is foolish. But once in a while I meet someone who gets it, and it's like I've found an old friend I'd never met. Like finding Jesus again. You live in the holy, and the holy gives everything else back. Every day is Easter."

In the gospel of John, just before death, Jesus says, "It is finished." That word, *finished*, also means *perfect, complete.*

Jesus' death is not his own. It belongs to all creation and all time, so the church has believed. All that is, dies with him. No use fighting anymore. The crack is revealed, and the breeze that blows through stirs up the scent of something new. Like lilies when you walk past.

Your struggle to keep that small company afloat on a sea of debt. That long battle with cancer. Those extended years of suspicion and blaming over the state of the church. Your loving fear or anxiety for the well-being of your children, or yearnings for children unfulfilled. That war with your body—with its cravings, or its failings, or its resistance. That wrestling with your soul—with its homelessness, or its silence, or its anger. Or that odd sense that settles in the bones that even the good times, when they come, just can't last. All of those things that speak of death in the way the world teaches death.

Fact is, they're finished. Over. You've already died and all creation and all time has died *with* you. So live in Easter-time, and do whatever you want in the new playground called re-creation or resurrection. Reflect Easter's light. Obey Easter's justice. Respond to Easter's love.

Make no doubt about it. Jesus died an actual death, in an actual place and at an actual moment in history. Brutally and unjustly executed by a group of people with religious, political, and military power. The ministry of Jesus and his followers during those remarkable three years of itinerant preaching and healing was finally shut down and finished, on the cross. Jesus' words seemed powerless before the authority of politics and religion, and the devotion of most of his followers was found empty when it all seemed to come tumbling down. The two Marys and Salome seem to be the notable exceptions.

But what does history know of real perfection, or of endings *beyond* endings?

The touch of the divine spied in Jesus, the trace that seemed erased on Good Friday appeared *again*. And we in the church say now, and have been saying for quite some time, that what was actually erased on Good Friday was not God at all, but was the world's efforts to maintain the lie that God cannot be known, and has not spoken. Truth re-imagined and concocted for gain, *that* God is over. And God, known in Jesus, begins again.

You see, the two Marys and Salome went to the tomb that morning…and found an angel waiting for them.

Yes, it had ended. And it had finally begun.

Oh sure, you say to me. It's easy to *talk* about this—about some new reality ready to break in, or about being raised out of the trials of this life. That's your job as a preacher. But talk is cheap, and it can even be destructive. After all, just this week we've been reading about this guy out near San Diego who'd been preaching about resurrection, and about leaving this earthy plane of challenge and effort, for years. He just led thirty-nine yearning people into a *real* finish, far more tangible than what you're talking about—plastic bags over their heads, purple cloths in shapes of triangles, and suitcases all packed. A mass suicide just this week, all from preaching resurrection! Leave us to our ordinary lives; they're much safer than this stuff. For if you ignore all the spaceship nonsense, wasn't this guy in San Diego preaching basically the same message you are?

No, he wasn't. The gospel we preach is something else altogether. For the resurrection scriptures, including the very ones you heard this morning, do not promise some magical lifting out from this world. And neither do the majority of ways in which these texts have been talked about during the past two millennia. The death of which they speak and the resurrection promise they display tie world history and God's history together; they wed the material and the spiritual in a way that is quite different from pie-in-the-sky schemes or otherworldly fantasies.

The resurrection scriptures, and the theologies they've sparked, speak to us about the spiritually actual results of an actually spiritual event. Christianity doesn't separate the material and the spiritual. Neither does it separate body and soul, as if the trick to a happy life were to overcome the battle of flesh and spirit by choosing one side over the other and going for all the gusto you can in whichever direction you choose. Neither spiritualism nor materialism is enough for us, since Easter.

For when we say that in Christ all things are complete, we are saying that once we give up our dreams of control, of pure pleasure, or of immortality in the things of life, the things of life are given back to us again—only now we know deep in our hearts that they have been given back to us not for mistaken uses, but for God's glory. We are saying that divisions we've been taught between the spiritual and the material are false, and that because all things are now new in Christ we needn't live in fear of *either* the spiritual *or* the material.

A Christian Palestinian peacemaker once told me the story in his own way: My people are on their own Via Dolorosa, he said,

> on the path that Jesus walked to his death. Some of us fight it with all we've got, and some of us give in and are overcome, and some of us bury the bitterness inside until it comes out in insane and destructive ways. But some of us know that Jesus already walked this path, and brought all of creation with him—us, and our enemies with us. It's

already finished. We know it, because Mary found the tomb empty. We know this. And because of it, we can act bravely not only for justice but also for reconciliation and peace. This is the work of the church, because of Easter.

A group of us from this congregation were visiting in the West Lawndale neighborhood of the city with Corla Hawkins, also known as Mamma Hawk, at her program called Recovering the Gift Child. There we heard the story again, in still another way. It was the meeting at which the idea of joining some of our Sunday school students with her students for a Christmas party was born. There we sat, hearing her story. We learned of the day five or six years ago when she challenged the principle of the neglected elementary school in which she was teaching: "Why do we have gifted children in this school who fail?" she asked. "The school's dead. Let me have those children, and let me do what I need to do, and I'll show you something new."

We learned that her bluff was called. And what then began in one room now takes up an entire wing of the school, with more than forty children under her care *making it*. Year round classes and gatherings. The children who don't have homes go home with her. The parents who need special help are given it. Demands are high, and the power of resurrection is harnessed.

"Jesus is spoken in every classroom," the sign says just inside the entrance. The day begins in prayer. The Bible is taught, with interpretations offered from several angles. Both students and teachers are called to live their lives as children of Jesus.

"In a public school?" we ask. "How can you do this? Don't they shut you down?"

"When they can assure me that they've taken Satan out of the school, I'll take Jesus out. But until then, I'm not spending sixteen hours a day in hell without my Jesus!...And you know," she went on, "this neighborhood has already died anyway. Nobody with power cares about us. We can do anything we want, because it's already over. We're dead as far as the world is concerned. So we can begin again. And I'll keep doing it until God tells me to stop."

By some measures, her comments seem calculating, even strategic. But filled by the Holy Spirit, they're more than some material move measuring possibilities on a graph of inner city politics.

No, no, no. They're a taste of Easter.

Honor and deal with the intangible things of life knowing that God is as touchable as the pews you feel with real hands or the pillow on which you laid your head last night. And treat the practical things of life for what they are in an Easter-filled reality—precious gifts of Christ's spirit to be cared for with a kind of resurrection joy.

Let me put it another way: *In Christian faith, the separation between here and there dies, and a transformed kind of life is born. The resurrection of Christ from the dead, and our witness to its power in a myriad of ways, binds the practical realities of ordinary living to the transforming, life-giving possibility that the God who has created all of this, and lived with it, and loved it, has shown it a new way—on the other side of death.*

Now does this make any *real* difference? It does for that young woman who died, in a way, during that field hockey practice. It does for that Palestinian priest. It does for each one of those children in Mamma Hawk's classroom. It does for each one of you who care to attend the feast. And it is the witness of the church through the ages, however clouded the church has been by its own folly, that it makes all the difference in the *world* for all the *difference* in the world.

My friends, it's over. Let it begin.

Amen.

5

"Remembrance and Imagination"

Peter J. Gomes

Rejoice in the Lord always: and again I say, Rejoice. Let your moderation be known unto all men. The Lord is at hand. Be careful for nothing; but in every thing by prayer and supplication with thanksgiving let your requests be made known unto God. And the peace of God, which passeth all understanding, shall keep your hearts and minds through Christ Jesus. Finally, brethren, whatsoever things are true, whatsoever things are honest, whatsoever things are just, whatsoever things are pure, whatsoever things are lovely, whatsoever things are of good report; if there be any virtue, and if there be any praise, think on these things. Those things, which ye have both learned, and received, and heard, and seen in me, do: and the God of peace shall be with you. (Phil. 4:4–9, KJV)

What are these "things" to which Paul commends our attention in our text for today? "All that is true, all that is noble, all that is just and pure, all that is lovely and gracious, whatever is excellent and admirable; fill all your thoughts with these things," he says.

My sermon this morning is something of a commencement address, filled with splendid and impossible advice and easily dismissed as "what one would say" on occasions such as this. Dean Sperry, my predecessor as Plummer Professor, once found himself standing on the platform of Williams College, watching the long procession draw near. While waiting, he glanced down at the program in his hand, and found to his complete surprise that he was listed as the commencement speaker. When asked later what he did and how he did it, he replied, "I said the usual things that one says on such occasions, and I said them three times."

The things that I will say this morning are among the "usual things" that one says—to graduating seniors especially—but because this is the last time that many of you are likely to hear them, at least in this place, and at least from me, for Paul's sake, for my sake, and most of all, for your sake, I invite you to listen, and to "think on these things."

Recently I have been rereading J.B. Phillips' translation of the New Testament, and as usual I find his version more engaging even than the King James Version. The King James Version says, "think on these things," but Phillips renders it, "Fill all your thoughts with these things," which is a very different way of putting it.

In the abstract, the "noble thoughts," as we might call them, seem cool and aloof, and removed from our everyday experience. There are at least two ways by which the temptation to abstraction can be avoided, both of which were familiar to Paul, and each of which worked for him and for the Philippians; and I suggest that they will work for you here and now. The first of these acts, to translate these noble thoughts from abstraction to life, is the act of remembrance; and the second is the act of imagination. On this Communion Sunday, this Festival of Pentecost, we are engaged in acts both of remembrance and of imagination. Let me try to translate them into the substance of our text.

Paul always invites his listeners to acts of remembrance, constantly reminding people to remember. "Remember what it was like before you knew Christ. Remember what it was like before I came to you. Remember what it was like when you were young in the faith, or frightened, or intimidated, or new." Even more, throughout all his writings, Paul invites people to remember their moments of victory, of achievement, of success, of pleasure, of satisfaction. He invites us to remember those precious moments in our lives. Remember what the Lord has done for you, remember what you have done for the Lord, remember what others have done for you, and remember what you have done for others. Memory is the great key to this enterprise.

One of the last rites for seniors in Harvard College is to remember, and many of you have been doing much remembering these last few days. In fact, for most of you seniors in Harvard College, the past is much clearer than the future, perhaps even clearer than the present. No tree, no gate, no pathway is without its capacity to evoke a memory, to make us remember. Sometimes you remember the bad stuff, an unpleasant encounter or two, bad work done in class or lab, moments when you behaved badly or were badly treated. To this very day I remember things that I wish I hadn't said to a college roommate now forty years ago, but by and large the memories that we invoke are good, and the act of remembering is very good indeed. These are moments of love, even of nobility, moments of joy and graciousness, moments in which justice and truth and virtue were experienced if only momentarily. We are to remember these moments because in them we find evidence of God's presence and activity in our lives. To remember is to be reminded, even in our loneliness, that we have never been alone, abandoned, or forgotten. It is the essence of religion to remember, for it is in recollection that we find out, that is, remember, or put back together again, how God has dealt with us; and in doing so we remember how on a rare occasion or two we too have acted nobly, responded graciously; and just as it will surprise you to discover how good God has been to you, it will also surprise you to discover those moments in your own young lives when you have exhibited these very qualities on which you are now called to think.

At the risk of stroking sufficiently large egos, let me say that you are probably better than you think you are. Better still, put it this way—at least one person somewhere remembers some act of noble kindness you have performed and have perhaps forgotten, it being too small for you to remember. Somebody, however, does; somebody knows how good you are, how kind you have been, how thoughtful you have been, and you know how good somebody else is. So when Paul says, "think on these things," I believe he means that we are to think not simply in abstraction, but in the frail flesh of our own human experience.

Acts of remembrance are keys to acts of imagination, and they are important too. If you can remember, you can imagine. If you can look backward with the rediscovery of things once lost but now recalled, surely you can look ahead with some imagination as to what might be. Paul's little list here in Philippians is not for the past alone but is a recipe for the future. These are the qualities on which we both think, and then act, our way into the future.

Let me illustrate what I mean by this. At about this time of the year, seniors in college are frequently asked, "What are you going to do next year? What are your plans?" It has become something of a rude question; it makes them nervous, and it makes us sound like all of their mothers put together, and at this point that is not a good thing. However, I have given up being sensitive on this point. Of course nobody knows what his or her own future is, even if there is a job at McKinsey or a fellowship at Cambridge or an admission to graduate school: you still do not know what the future holds. The reverse is also true: those of you who have no plans beyond lunch today must remember—to quote a famous book—that there is a plan for you with your name on it, and it will find you when you and it are ready. So, all I have to say to you, you overindulgent anxious seniors, is relax, every one of you! As Paul has said in our lesson, "Be anxious for nothing"; that is, you can't control everything, so be anxious for nothing.

The real question to you is not whether you have a job or a plan, but whether you have an imagination. Can you think of anything beyond the moment? What do you imagine life will hold for you? What do you want life to hold for you? Anybody can see what is there. Anybody can go where a map will take them. Seeing what isn't there, however, traveling without a map, is what makes life interesting, and that is what the imagination is all about. It is the use of the imagination that sets the spirit free. It is the use of imagination that allows the Holy Spirit—that we celebrate today—to be set free in each and every one of us, giving us the appearance at times of being drunk and out of control and without a plan, and yet it is that very spirit-filled imagination that sets us free.

Perhaps some of you saw the *Globe*'s feature last week, in which a number of us were asked what we would be doing in life if we weren't doing what we are doing. Many of my friends, perhaps even some of you, were shocked by my reply. Never in my wildest imagination, and I have a very wild and fertile imagination, had I imagined that I would have spent the past thirty-one years here among you. That was neither a plausible plan nor even a reasonable fantasy. No! I had imagined something better for myself than this. I imagined myself first as curator of American Decorative Arts and then eventually as director of the Museum of Fine Arts here in Boston. The man on the telephone asked, "Did you imagine yourself starting out as director?" I said, "Oh no, but I'd be director by now, I assure you." I wanted to be both curator and director wrapped up in one.

To some of you this might seem an instance of a bad plan, a thwarted ambition, an unrealistic expectation, a dangerous fantasy, but I do not offer it as any of the above. I offer it as an example of the claims of the imagination on the future and proof that the future had a claim on me. They were not one and the same; it was an amazing coincidence that "my" plan was trumped by "the" plan, and it only goes to show that there is a plan, whether or not you know it. In that plan, as Paul would say, we are meant to imagine, indeed to construct, a world in which all that is true, all that is noble, all that is just and pure, all that is lovable and gracious, whatever is excellent and admirable, may flourish…at least in us. You must be able to imagine a world, and your place in it, where this may be so. Remembering your past, imagining your future—these are good acts for your last rites.

How, however, will we get from here to there? A few verses later in our text, Paul gives the answer when he utters the now-famous lines: "I can do all things through Christ who strengthens me" (Phil. 4:13). The road to the future, passing through imagination and remembrance, is the road by which Christ leads us from today to the day after tomorrow. Those are words of empowerment; those are words of enablement. They make all things possible through Christ, who strengthens us.

You may have noticed that we have some very visible and audible young visitors in these front pews this morning, and I have a word to you parents and godparents on behalf of these children: unless they are even smarter than you think they are, they will not remember much of what happens today, and even less of what I have to say. Their memory will depend on you. You will remind them of what happened, but you must be able to imagine for them today what their future will be. There is a plan for each and every one of them, with each one's name on it, and your job, parents, is not to get in the way, but to let God have God's way with these children, which, with Christ, will enable them to do everything and anything through Christ, who strengthens them. Your children must have the benefit of your spiritual imagination now in order that the future into which we will shortly welcome them will be one in which they rejoice.

These words remind us that we are not on our own, and that as we are we can do nothing. Paul was not deficient in the ego department. Remember Churchill's famous remark on Clement Atlee? "He is a modest man because he has much about which to be modest." Paul is more Churchill than Atlee, but even he recognizes that on his own he is nothing, and with Christ, who strengthens him, all things are possible—or imaginable.

Here's a fact you may find hard to take, but I find it instructive. Think of this: Christ did not change Paul's world. Think of that. Christ did not change one thing in Paul's world. The Romans still ran the show, the Jews and Greeks were still difficult, life was still nasty, brutish, and short; death was certain and often painful. None of those facts was changed or mitigated. What Christ changed was Paul's imagination, and by doing that he empowered him, enabled him to live as a changed man in an unchanged world. That would not have been possible for Paul on his own, but only with the power of Christ in him, the power of the Holy Spirit whose gift we celebrate today, allowing him to remember, to imagine, and finally, to persevere, carrying as realities the impossibility of these things about which he asks us to think: "All that is true, all that is noble, all that is just and pure, all that is lovable and gracious, whatever is excellent and admirable"—in a sordid, shabby world, dumbed down and tuned out, we are meant to "fill all [our] thoughts with these things"—these noble thoughts.

I will give you my definition of what a Christian is. To be a Christian is to be a changed man or a changed woman in an unchanged world.

Vocation

6

Our Work Is More than a Job

Alison L. Boden

"Always rejoice in the good work that you do," wrote Thomas Aquinas. "I would if only I could figure out what good work *to* do!" would many young (and not so young) people respond. Indeed, the choice of one's life's work is one of the great questions that fill and define the journey from youth to adulthood. The choice does not come to everyone, however. Poverty, family tradition or expectations, or the constrictions of a society may make choice of occupation a distinct privilege. Those who do have choices often think that their first decision will be their last. Gone are those days! In these times one may look forward not only to changing companies or locations within a field but also to changing professions entirely—and repeatedly. How fortunate are those who can look back over new directions chosen throughout the years and see the course of their life as having an unbroken line, despite the endings and fresh starts. The oxbows and steep curves, in retrospect, appear as the most interesting, if most challenging or unstable, of times. Old choices are not seen as a waste of time or years but as necessary and proper stages on a good road of self-discovery and response to God.

Some years ago a good friend, the benefits officer for the university at which I served as chaplain, mentioned that many faculty members had answered a questionnaire about "how many hours per week do you work" with numbers such as eighty or ninety. She chuckled, saying that the question was meant only to determine whether respondents were full-time or half-time. I flinched to realize that my own answer had been eighty. We spend many of our waking hours at work, both paid and unpaid. Some of us, because of the demands of our job or our demands of ourselves, spend the majority of our waking hours at work. Students are not wrong to think that any occupational choice they make will have serious ramifications for their quality of life, regardless of the income they earn.

The implications are serious on many levels. One study has shown that 95 percent of all Americans report that they hate their work. The highest incidence of heart attacks in this country occurs between 8:00 and 9:00 on Monday mornings. Too many of us are so stressed by our work, it would seem, that it literally kills us. Thomas Merton has written, "The rush and pressure of modern life are a form, perhaps the most common form, of its innate violence."[1] Such violence may be rarely discussed, but it is often perceived. Challenging work, in itself, is not bad; it can bring us discovery, meaning, growth, and adventure. However, the work that expects too much, that denies workers a life outside of work even when they are at home, that exploits, that belittles or dehumanizes—this is the work that stresses unto death, physical death or spiritual death. Genesis 2:15 describes the origin of work as a curse.

Or perhaps it is not work that is curse but rather toil, the sweat of the brow; some fortunate people experience even the most physically and spiritually demanding work not as draining but as life-giving. It is hard but never toilsome. Their bodies may be exhausted by their labor but their souls are reinvigorated in direct proportion with the energy they expend. The hard work they do is a source of nourishment, is rich with a sense of purpose, and carries rewards never measurable on spreadsheets. It draws on

---

[1]Thomas Merton, *Conjectures of a Guilty Bystander* (Garden City, N.Y.: Doubleday, 1966).

gifts rather than competencies and pushes the laborer to make self-discoveries on issues, and along paths, of integrity and conviction. In Zora Neale Hurston's *Their Eyes Were Watching God*, Janie says to Pheoby, "Ah wants tuh utilize mahself all ovah." She's not alone! How many of us want to spend all our days utilizing ourselves all over—not just the sequestered moments in which we feed our souls on the worship of God and love of children and thrilling to music and literature and film and friends, but the significant portion of our lives devoted to the demands of our work. We want work that draws out the creative juices from every corner of our minds, hearts, and spirits, that summons more from us than we even knew we had and maybe even teaches us that we are larger souls than we thought we were. How wonderful to have work that utilizes us all over, that draws on and nurtures our gifts. Such labor is not just work at all but rather *vocation*.

Vocare—"calling" in Latin—is the root of the word. How different is that work to which we are obligated from the work to which we are called! Often the criteria of our calling are beyond our articulation. We know that we must have a lurking vocation; could God create anyone without any gifts, mission, or purpose, no matter how humble? Toward the end of his life, F. Scott Fitzgerald wrote to his editor and old friend, "In a small way I was an original."[2] For many of us the search for what we uniquely may contribute is interwoven with our question of calling, the search for the vocation through which we can give expression to our originality. Without hubris, many people know themselves to have some word or deed of truth to share, especially young adults as their world opens up to new thinkers and old questions, other cultures and belief systems. Certainly some vocation exists by which, first, to discover their unique voice and, second, to share it with the world?

A helpful question to some young people as they discern their calling, one that reroutes their practical thinking about professions, is "Who do you want to be?" as a substitute (or precursor) for "What do you want to be?" The answers are wide-ranging, and often touching: I want to be a person of honor. I want to be known for generosity. I want to be known as fair. I want to stand for justice. I want to live out an ethic of mercy and compassion. I want to be

---

[2]Roy Pearson, "The Implications of Our High Calling," *The Living Pulpit* 5, no. 3, (July-Sept. 1996).

someone who sees the face of God in everyone I meet. Sometimes the vocational answers are beatitudinally transformed: the person who says she wants to see God in others realizes that she wants to be one of those "who see God." The one who wants to stand for justice realizes that he wants to hunger and thirst for righteousness. Some understand that they want to become "the merciful," or the peacemakers, or the children of God. Have they stopped talking about banking or law or real estate or parenting or writing or the ministry? Not at all. But they've begun to explore ways to imbue whatever they do (and pray God it will be fulfilling!) with a warm sense of calling that may transform their profession into their vocation. The New Testament declares the vocation of every Christian simply to be the living out of the gospel. The calling is not always simple, of course, and can lead us to places we never dreamed we'd find ourselves and to people we never knew to love. The courage needed so to incarnate the Christian vocation is possible only through faith in God's presence, hope for God's future, and the felt accompaniment of the cloud of witnesses who also heed the call.

And so the question of vocation comes to be understood not so much as an issue of what we do but how and why. What do we understand the purpose and end of our labor to be? How is it a response to God? Eight centuries ago, Julian of Norwich wrote,

> Be a gardener.
> Dig a ditch,
> toil and sweat,
> and turn earth upside down
> and seek deepness
> and water plants in time.
> Continue this labor
> and make sweet floods to run
> and noble and abundant fruits
> to spring.
> Take this food and drink
> and carry it to God
> as your true worship.[3]

---

[3]Julian of Norwich, *Revelation of Divine Love*, chapter 51. For a more recent translation, see Julian of Norwich, *Showings*, trans. Edmund Colledge and James Walsh (New York: Paulist Press, 1978), 273.

It's no call to community gardening as such but a call to a society then overwhelmingly engaged in agriculture, as are the great majority of people today in two-thirds of the world, to view the sweat of their brow as a love-offering to God. Beyond grape and grain, our obvious gifts of the earth processed to the altar, all that we produce is offered to God as a sacrifice of praise. The dirt under our nails, the hours spent over a hoe (or for us the keyboard, broom, or spreadsheet) are offered up, a tribute, a contribution to a creation that God first called good and now asks us to heal. When our sweat-offering becomes our love-offering, our work cannot define us but we define our work. When the labor we must perform becomes the service we feel called to perform, we have transformed our work into our vocation. We have found a quiet way to love God with all our heart, soul, mind, and strength even—or especially—during those many hours of the day and week that we labor.

As we spend our days exercising our own vocations, it is good to be mindful that we are, simultaneously, the very vocation of another. We are the testimony of another's calling. We are the works of God, the love-offering of the labor of God who tilled soil and dust and shaped and molded and made all that is and each of us. We are the works of Christ and of the sweat of his calling to redeem and to transform. We are the works of the Spirit, who labors in every second and place to lead us into all freedom. We are the fruit of God's creative vocation, of Christ's redemptive vocation, of the Spirit's sustaining vocation.

Our own vocations are linked to these. The central question behind our labor is not one of task but of perspective. The works of our days become large and small testimonies to the reign of God, to an in-breaking reality, one to which we not only testify with our labors but also actively create. Our work is never in vain if it points to God's reign, if it bears witness to the good news of God's new heaven and new earth. Repetitive or dull, thrilling or mundane, the chance to transform our labor into witness is always before us. Meister Eckhart wrote, "The outward work can never be small if the inward one is great, and the outward work can never be great or good if the inward is small or of little worth."

These are ordinary days, the usual, nameless days of busily getting things done in the company of good people (and maybe some who are mean). The ordinary days of working do not feel very significant in the grand scheme. We sleep, we eat, we chat, we relax, and we work long and hard. But these days have, if we can find our vocation in them, a quiet sense of purpose and of praise. They are just another workday, a day of dirt under the nails, of sensing the Spirit's subtle presence in the diapers and the hallways and the computer screen. These are the days that fill up most of our lives—days of building, days of testimony, days of blessing.

7

"The Big Exam"

Wayne A. Meeks

This sermon was preached in Battell Chapel at Yale University on Reformation Sunday, October 27, 1996.

When the Pharisees heard that he had silenced the Sadducees, they gathered together, and one of them, a lawyer, asked him a question to test him. "Teacher, which commandment in the law is the greatest?" He said to him, "'You shall love the Lord your God with all your heart, and with all your soul, and with all your mind.' This is the greatest and first commandment. And a second is like it: 'You shall love your neighbor as yourself.' On these two commandments hang all the law and the prophets."

Now while the Pharisees were gathered together, Jesus asked them this question: "What do you think of the Messiah? Whose son is he?" They said to him, "The son of David." He said to them, "How is it then that David by the Spirit calls him Lord, saying,

> 'The Lord said to my Lord,
> "Sit at my right hand,
> until I put your enemies under your feet"'?

If David thus calls him Lord, how can he be his son?" No
one was able to give him an answer, nor from that day did
anyone dare to ask him any more questions.
(Mt. 22:34–46)

It was a test, says Matthew. The one who asked was, after all,
a lawyer, so what would one expect? This was a hostile test, as
Matthew makes plain, for he has gathered into this chapter a series
of stories about Jesus' opponents trying "to trap him by his speech"
(v. 15). "Teacher," they say, "tell us your opinion. Is it right to pay
the tribute to Caesar?" A no-win question, as intended. An answer
must mark Jesus either as a revolutionary or as a traitor to the
national hopes of his people. "Show me a coin," he replies. "Whose
image and whose inscription are those?" "Caesar's." "Well, then,"
he says, "give to Caesar what is Caesar's, but give to God what is
God's." The Pharisees and Herodians withdraw, astounded. The
Sadducees take up the interrogation. "Teacher, suppose a woman
whose husband dies when they are childless. Following the law
of Moses, she marries his brother and, when he dies, another
brother, until in all she has been wife of seven brothers. If there is
a resurrection, as you claim, whose wife will she be?" "You," says
Jesus, "know neither the scriptures nor the power of God."

"And when the Pharisees heard that he had stumped the
Sadducees," they tried again. One of them, a lawyer, to test him
inquires, "Teacher, which of the commandments in the Torah is
the big one?" We know that line. "Teacher, what are the really
important parts of this book you assigned?" "Teacher, will this be
on the final exam?" Life, and knowledge, are complicated. We
crave simplicity: the one-liner, the sound-bite. We watch the
debate, waiting for the one big gaffe that will let us say who won.
"Teacher, which is the big one?" The Torah is complicated. Later
rabbis calculated it contained 365 negative commandments and
248 positive ones. A Gentile came to the great teacher Shammai,
the story goes, and demanded, "Rabbi, teach me the Torah while
standing on one foot." Shammai drove him away with a stick.
When the same Gentile came to Shammai's rival Hillel with the
same demand, Hillel replied more gently: "What you do not want
to be done to you do not do to another. That is the whole of the

Torah—all else is commentary—now go and study." There is nothing wrong with aiming for simplicity at the center of things. And we are only too familiar with questions that put one to the test.

But if we were able to test Jesus, I think we'd want to ask a different question. I'd want to ask, "Teacher, in this world filled with corruption and bounded by death, defeating our hopes and confounding our understanding, can you make me believe that there is a God?"

No one in Matthew's gospel asks that question. The question is only, given God, what does God require of us? Almost never in the Bible is our question addressed, "Is there a God?" The Bible begins with the God who is there, before anything, beyond all things. A God who confronts the man and the woman hiding their nakedness in the garden. A God who calls: "Abraham, Abraham, go from your land and your father's house." "Moses, Moses, come, I will send you to Pharaoh." A God who issues commands, establishes covenants, rewards, and punishes. A God who surprises: "Lo, I am doing a deed in your days which you would not believe if someone told you." The Bible assumes that God is not a possibility about which we can decide, but a power that simply is, a voice that simply speaks, a presence from whom one cannot hide. A God who is principal actor in layer upon layer of stories, but a God not easily caught in the net cast by the sort of questions we ask when we are testing or being tested. The world of the Bible, in which this God intrudes with comings and calls and commands, is for most of us now a strange and distant world. From that world we hear the lawyer's simple but tricky question, asking for the simple but revealing answer: "Which commandment is the big one in the Torah?"

Jesus plays the game. A simple answer: "You shall love the Lord your God with your whole heart and with your whole soul and with your whole mind: this is the big and first commandment." Jesus answers the way one ought to answer a lawyer, by quoting the law. He quotes the Shema, recited twice a day by every observant Jew. In Mark's version of the story, he quotes more fully and more in accord with the Hebrew original: "Hear, O Israel: the Lord our God, the Lord is one. And you shall love the Lord your God from the whole of your heart and from the whole of your soul and from the whole of your strength" (Mk. 12:29–30, author's translation). Now the Hebrew original spoke of "heart" (*lvav*), "soul" or "life-force" (*nefesh*), and "capacity" or "power" (*me'od*). Matthew omits the preface and, oddly, changes Mark's translation, leaving out "strength" and substituting "mind." In the Hebrew Bible, the word for "heart" refers not only to the physical organ but also to the center of both emotion and intellect. In effect, Matthew has chosen to give us a double translation of that word: both "heart" and "mind." Why has Matthew chosen to emphasize the mental side of Jesus' quotation?

For one thing, this whole chapter, Matthew 22, is a battle of minds. It shows Jesus as the artist of the perfect squelch. One after another, the different groups of his opponents put trick questions to him, and he answers with such wit and precision that they are left speechless and dumbfounded. To cap it all off, when they have all given up in confusion, *he* sets *them* a question: "Who is the Messiah? If he is David's son, how can David call him Lord?" He gives them a riddle; they have no reply. As a matter of fact, the scene is artificial. The Jews of Jesus' time had many different notions about a messiah or a prophet or a priest of the end-time. It is the Christians who narrow it down to a single figure, heaping all of these titles on Jesus. So, ironically, we are more likely than the historical scribes to create a doctrinal box into which the actions of God's messenger had to fit. Never mind: it is clear that Matthew writes for a community that felt itself dangerously threatened by the emerging new institutions cobbled together by scribes and Pharisees after the Romans had destroyed the temple. Matthew's portrait of Jesus here is a very polemical one, and for the moment we can ignore that polemic.

What we cannot ignore is the answer Jesus gives to his questioner. It is an utterly simple answer, as demanded. Watch out, though. Jesus' simple answers tend to have a catch to them. Remember the story parallel to this one, in which the young man runs up to Jesus to ask, "Teacher, what good thing must I do in order to inherit eternal life?" "Keep the commandments," says he. "I've done that," says the youth; "what more?" A simple thing: "Sell everything you have, give the money to the poor, and come, follow me."

So here, too, the simplicity is mockingly deceptive, isn't it? All you have to do is to love God with your whole heart, your whole soul, your whole mind. What on earth does that mean? How can that be possible? How can we, as people of a university, love God with our whole mind?

What it cannot mean is a blind submission of the mind to authority, whether authority of an individual leader, an institution, a book, or a tradition. This is Reformation Sunday, in Protestant churches, and it is well for us to remember once again the dramatic words of Martin Luther as he stood before the Diet of Worms in 1521, which are still a charter of freedom for those of us who stand in that tradition:

> "Since then your Majesty and your lordships desire a simple reply, [Luther said], I will answer without horns and without teeth. Unless I am convicted by Scripture and plain reason—I do not accept the authority of popes and councils, for they have contradicted each other—my conscience is captive to the Word of God. I cannot and I will not recant anything, for to go against conscience is neither right nor safe. God help me."

If loving God with all my mind were to mean sacrificing the best that the mind tells me on the altar of what "everybody knows," or "common sense," or "what must be believed," or what someone tells me "the Bible says," then I would find somewhere in the heart or in the soul an unease, a reservation, an offense to the wholeness of love that would destroy love. To love God with the *whole* of our minds is plain contrary to that sacrifice of intellect that religious demagogues demand.

To make that assertion, however, does not mean that wherever my reasoning may lead me I will find *truth!* We know only too well how often our reasoning becomes rationalization, how easily we deceive ourselves, how heartlessly we can pursue the goal of testing, and proving, and controlling knowledge. Indeed, one of the questions that plague those of us who spend our lives in and around universities is whether we can so devote ourselves to the life of the mind as it seems we must, if we are to thrive here, without losing our heart and our soul. Does Jesus' reply to the tester offer us any help with that? Yes, in three ways, I think.

First, the three metaphors of our life's centering are held together: the whole heart, the whole soul, the whole mind. We are not allowed to choose among them. There is an "emotional intelligence," as we have been reminded lately by a widely praised book. The mind is not located exclusively in the upper brain. "The heart has its reasons," Pascal said, "that reason knows not at all."

Second, what we are to do with heart, soul, and mind is to *love.* Imagine a mind in love! But look around you: in this place and every place of learning, the best of our scholars, the best of our teachers, the best of our students are all minds in love. Do you not see how they pursue the hidden fact, the furtive explanation, the hidden cause—with all the passion with which ever a lover pursued the beloved? The scientist running the experiment one more time as night stretches toward dawn. The ethnographer patiently waiting and writing while the tribal elder explains once again his people's stories and their doings and what their ancestors' ancestors told them of the world. The painter laboring to find just the right juxtaposition of colors, just the strokes of brush and knife, to enable those of duller vision to see what she has seen in the deeper landscape of the imagination. All these are moved by more than curiosity—rather by a passion for knowing, for understanding, for revealing. You do not have to be either a Platonist or a romantic to see that they are all lovers.

Yet most of them would be more than puzzled if you suggested they were loving *God* with their minds. Chances are a fair number of them would say they are atheists or agnostics. The latter are likely right to disbelieve in most of what passes for talk about God in our degraded public discourse today. No matter: the kind of passionate knowing I am talking about inevitably takes one beyond such talk and toward the one we stammeringly name God and image by our inadequate metaphors. Everyone who loves with the whole mind, a mind not torn away from the whole heart and soul, everyone who loves the world in all its complexity, all its horror, all its glory, loves with a love that presses toward the one who transcends that world and our knowledge of it. To love with the *whole* mind is, I believe, to love God willy-nilly, whether ever naming that name or not, whether aware or not.

And the third thing Jesus does in his answer is to throw in a second commandment for free. "Love God: that's the big, the first commandment," he says, "And there's a second that's like it: You shall love your neighbor as yourself. From these two hang the whole of the Law and the Prophets." This second commandment is like the first, says Jesus. How so? Loving the neighbor is like loving God and is the everyday way we love God. "If you do not love your brother or sister whom you have seen," asks another New Testament writer, "how can you love God, whom you have not seen?" The troubling part is that "as yourself," which echoes the earlier phrase, "with the whole heart, the whole soul, the whole mind." That makes us squirm here in the ivory tower. With all the things we have to do just to get through this place, if we are students, or to stay in this place, if we are faculty or staff, it's pretty hard to make much time for the neighbors. We can squeeze in a few hours of volunteer work—which after all will look good on the résumé—but that "as yourself" seems to demand something more than that.

It is good that we feel some tension between this commandment and the self-centeredness that the academic routine seems bound to impose on us. It is good that our consciences are not easy when we pass the homeless people on York or Wall or Chapel. It is good that there is some competition between our obligation to devote our whole minds to the job of scholarship and our obligation to love the inconvenient and unlovely people who just happen to share our world. But these ways of thinking about our duty and our limitations tend to pull apart just those things in our life that Jesus' saying wants to keep together: the wholeness of heart, soul, and mind; the likeness of loving God and loving neighbor.

The real question here is one of vocation. An old-fashioned word: we prefer to talk of our careers. The real question is not whether we can spare some time from our careers to love our neighbors; it is whether we have a vocation such that the best of our time and energy is engaged in a life lived for the neighbor. What are we doing all this learning for? Do we break our heads over these books and these experiments only so that we can have more power? More income? More satisfaction in the grand perfection of our inner selves? Or do we heed the word of Jesus, that to love God with all our minds is also to love the neighbor as ourselves? Can our intellectual labors be not only for knowledge's sake but also for the neighbor's sake?

This would not mean that only those inquiries that have immediate practical and social consequences would be pursued by the lover of God. Far from it. It may be precisely the whole-minded pursuit of pure science, just the dogged search for meaning in the small, apparently irrelevant detail of a past event, the obsession with the hidden meaning of an obscure poet long dead—it may be just these "irrelevant" devotions that will make the largest gifts to the neighbor in the long run. The question is rather whether we might yet recover something of that other great

Reformation doctrine, the doctrine of vocation. Christians all, not just priests, not just monks and nuns, do not have careers; they have a calling. Each of us is *called*, summoned by God to serve in the world in a unique way that will engage our whole heart, our whole soul, and our whole mind.

8

"What Are You Doing after Graduation?"

William H. Willimon

This sermon was offered at the 2001 Baccalaureate Service of Duke University.

> Then Joseph said to his brothers, "Come closer to me."
> And they came closer. He said, "I am your brother, Joseph,
> whom you sold into Egypt. And now do not be distressed,
> or angry with yourselves, because you sold me here; for
> God sent me before you to preserve life. For the famine
> has been in the land these two years; and there are five
> more years in which there will be neither plowing nor
> harvest. God sent me before you to preserve for you a
> remnant on earth, and to keep alive for you many
> survivors. So it was not you who sent me here, but God
> sent me before you to preserve life." (Gen. 45:4–8a)

Dear Duke Class of 2001. Graduation speakers are fond of extolling the great things you will do after graduation. Your great achievements at Duke are only a beginning. With a Duke education, you can do anything. Wall Street, Pennsylvania Avenue, or Rodeo Drive are breathlessly awaiting you to do that thing that you do, with them.

Because I know you, I know that you know not to swallow all graduation rhetoric. You've had psychology. There you discovered that most of you are that which has been done to you rather than by you. What you thought was your courageous, independent decision was, in reality, your mama's manipulation. Thank you, psychology.

The slogans of my generation were liberation, do your own thing, autonomy, even as a century of social science said that we are caught, jerked around by psychological, sociological, economic forces beyond our control.

In my First-Year-Student Seminar, we presented the case of Dave, in his early twenties, who, after carousing in a bar, despite his friends' efforts, got into a car and on his way home killed a child. The question: "Who was responsible?" Assign percentages of responsibility. Dave? His parents (both of whom were alcoholics)? His friends? The bartender? Society?

About a third of the class assigned 70 percent of the responsibility to Dave's parents. I was chagrined, as a parent, to see us take the rap for Dave.

A third of the class apportioned responsibility between the bartender and Dave's friends for not wrestling him to the ground and getting the car keys. About a third of the class insisted on a new category: Genetics. Studies show a genetic propensity toward alcohol abuse. Dave's genes did it.

And these were the same people who had declared, just the class before, that *they decided* to be at Duke!

Oh we prattle on nostalgically, "I am the captain of my fate, the master of my soul." But in our enlightened, twenty-first century moments, we admit there is a caughtness to us, jerked around by forces over which we have little control. Decisions made for us rather than by us account for us. You're here thinking about your marvelous undergraduate achievements, while Mom thinks, "I've done a good job on that one!"

Now we may quibble over what percentage of us our parents should take responsibility for. Okay, 20 percent of me is master of my fate, captain of my soul. But mostly we are the result of psychology, economics, genetics, or that which we have been able heroically to seize from external determinism.

Our culture tells us two stories. *One story* is that you are free, autonomous, who you choose to be. Which, as I have noted, flies in the face of just about everything the social sciences have taught. (Spinoza said, "If a rock could think, and if you threw that rock across a river, that rock would think that it was crossing the river because it wanted to.")

The other story says you are fixed, determined at birth, caught. Or, as one of you told me, when I asked the big question, "What are you doing after graduation?"

"My mom is a banker. Dad is a banker. I was doomed. Hello DeutscheBank."

Against these stories of who you are and where you are going, I want to place a third. It is from Genesis, out of Israel's past. I won't recount the whole thing, but I will say that Joseph, who grew up in a more dysfunctional family than any of you, is sold into Egyptian slavery by his brothers. But he lands on his feet at Pharaoh's place. Joseph is put in charge of all of the Pharaoh's public works. During a great famine, Joseph's brothers (who had attempted to kill him, then sold him into slavery) show up in Egypt looking for food. They do not know that the Egyptian official who stands before them, holding their family's life in his hands, the one before whom they grovel for food, is none other than little brother Joseph, the same kid brother they tried to get rid of earlier. This is where we come in. Little brother Joseph reveals himself to his older siblings. And when they realize that this great official standing before them is none other than little brother Joseph whom they had so terribly wronged, they are filled with fear. It is payback time, when little brother Joseph will get revenge for all his brothers did to him, the part of the story so dearly beloved by little sisters and brothers everywhere.

But Joseph calms their fears and tells them that though they deserve it, he is not going to get revenge. Rather he will bless them, give them the food they need. The family will be preserved. Then Joseph says something to his brothers that I want you to note. Looking back on what has happened over the years, all twists and turns, the weird events and strange coincidences, the heartache, the hurt, Joseph says, *"You meant this for evil. But God meant this for good. You didn't send me here. God sent me."*

Surprise! There is another actor in this story. As it turns out, the protagonists are not limited to Joseph, his brothers, and what he did or didn't do to them. There is a third participant without whom the story cannot be fully told: God. Joseph's brothers were meaning all of this for evil, to do in their uppity little brother, and Joseph was meaning simply to survive. But God was also busy, making meaning in the story that was not exclusively of Joseph's or his brothers' doing.

So Joseph declares, "You meant this for evil, but God meant this for good."

As modern people, we have been conditioned to describe our lives as mostly what we do, or mostly what is done to us by others. I am the sum of my choices. Or I am the sum of my genetic heritage. But this ancient story dares to assert another actor. Or more properly, an author. Our lives may not be stories written by us, or even by our parents, or our genes. Maybe there is a meaning beyond the meaning that we make. There is an author, unseen but nevertheless active. God.

So Joseph said, "You meant this for evil, but God meant this for good."

It raises a question: What if your life is not just yours? What if it's not your parents'?

I have seen this among you. Some of you have taken twists and turns, odd lurches to the left or to the right, that simply cannot be explained by reference to your psychological makeup or your sociological background. It is as if someone, something got hold of you, moved you to some new place not of your own devising.

People of faith tend to explain this inexplicable phenomenon by reference to God. Maybe we're actors in a play, and the playwright is greater than ourselves.

Augustine once said that when you look back over your life, the steps you have taken can first appear like chicken tracks in the mud, little chicken tracks going this way and that in the muddy chicken yard, without direction. But through the eyes of faith, sometimes those seemingly purposeless tracks take on pattern, direction. We begin to see that they are going somewhere. They suggest the hand of God. And it is then that you realize that the life you're living, the meaning that you mean, is not all that there is. We are busy, meaning this for evil, or for our selfish ambition, but God is busy meaning this for good.

The great commencement question must be reframed. It is too simple to ask, "What are you doing after graduation?"

A more complex, faithful question, "What is *God* doing with you after graduation?"

There is an old theological word for it: *Providence*. That time you are able, as Joseph was, to look back on your life, maybe by your twentieth reunion, and see that the times, the bad times as well as the good, had in them a sense of direction. While you were busy making your choices and decisions, God was also busy. Weaving. Creating.

I know somebody who is incredibly smart in physics. "Were your parents good in physics?" I asked.

"No."

"It is great that you have such an aptitude for physics," I said, "and that you have developed it so well."

"True," you said, "It's also a great responsibility. I have been given a gift. A lot is expected of me."

I thought that you had it just about right. There is a claim on you. We have a word for it. *Vocation.*

What the world calls mere natural endowments, are gifts. Every gift is also an assignment. Or as the poet Maya Angelou told you, right here, during your first week at Duke, "We have given you everything this society has, the best of it. You are the beneficiaries of the best of our educational system...*Now you owe us!*"

Keep looking over your shoulder as you go forth. Be open to the possibility of an unseen hand. The life you live may not be exclusively your own.

So congratulations, dear graduates. God has done great things through you, given great gifts, and means to do greater things even yet.

There is a claim on your life. You live not just for yourself. We have a word for it.

Vocation.

9

"Fear Not: Follow Me"

Ruthanna B. Hooke

Rev. Ruthanna Hooke preached this sermon at St. Paul's Episcopal Church in Wallingford, Connecticut, on February 4, 2001.

Now the angel of the LORD came and sat under the oak at Ophrah, which belonged to Joash the Abiezrite, as his son Gideon was beating out wheat in the wine press, to hide it from the Midianites. The angel of the LORD appeared to him and said to him, "The LORD is with you, you mighty warrior." Gideon answered him, "But sir, if the LORD is with us, why then has all this happened to us? And where are all his wonderful deeds that our ancestors recounted to us, saying, 'Did not the LORD bring us up from Egypt?' But now the LORD has cast us off, and given us into the hand of Midian." Then the LORD turned to him and said, "Go in this might of yours and deliver Israel from the hand of Midian; I hereby commission you." He responded, "But sir, how can I deliver Israel? My clan is the weakest in Manasseh, and I am the least in my family." The LORD said to him, "But I will be with you, and you shall strike down the Midianites, every one of them." Then he said to him, "If now I have found favor with you, then show me a sign that it is you who speak with me. Do not depart from here until I come to you, and bring out my present, and set it before you." And he said, "I will stay until you return."

So Gideon went into his house and prepared a kid, and unleavened cakes from an ephah of flour; the meat he put in a basket, and the broth he put in a pot, and brought them to him under the oak and presented them. The angel of God said to him, "Take the meat and the unleavened cakes, and put them on this rock, and pour out the broth." And he did so. Then the angel of the LORD reached out the tip of the staff that was in his hand, and touched the meat and the unleavened cakes; and fire sprang up from the rock and consumed the meat and the unleavened cakes; and the angel of the LORD vanished from his sight. Then Gideon perceived that it was the angel of the LORD; and Gideon said, "Help me, Lord GOD! For I have seen the angel of the LORD face to face." But the LORD said to him, "Peace be to you; do not fear, you shall not die." Then Gideon built an altar there to the LORD, and called it, The LORD is peace. (Judg. 6:11–24a)

Once while Jesus was standing beside the lake of Gennesaret, and the crowd was pressing in on him to hear the word of God, he saw two boats there at the shore of the lake; the fishermen had gone out of them and were washing their nets. He got into one of the boats, the one belonging to Simon, and asked him to put out a little way from the shore. Then he sat down and taught the crowds from the boat. When he had finished speaking, he said to Simon, "Put out into the deep water and let down your nets for a catch." Simon answered, "Master, we have worked all night long but have caught nothing. Yet if you say so, I will let down the nets." When they had done this, they caught so many fish that their nets were beginning to break. So they signaled their partners in the other boat to come and help them. And they came and filled both boats, so that they began to sink. But when Simon Peter saw it, he fell down at Jesus' knees, saying, "Go away from me,

Lord, for I am a sinful man!" For he and all who were with him were amazed at the catch of fish that they had taken; and so also were James and John, sons of Zebedee, who were partners with Simon. Then Jesus said to Simon, "Do not be afraid; from now on you will be catching people." When they had brought their boats to shore, they left everything and followed him. (Lk. 5:1–11)

Two images from our gospel story are vivid in my mind's eye. One is the boat pulling in onto the sandy shore, full to the gunwales, almost awash, brimming over with heaps of fish—shimmering, shining, their scales catching the dawn light, cascades of them pouring out onto the sands. More than anyone had ever seen before. And the second image: Peter, down on his knees on the beach, his strong hands up in front of his face as if to ward off a blow or shield them from a painfully bright light, as he looks up in terror at the man in front of him and says, "Depart from me, O Lord, for I am a sinful man."

Recently I was talking to some friends about what the Bible meant when it talked about "the fear of the Lord." We all agreed that the notion made no sense. It would make sense to be afraid of God if you believed that God was cruel, or angry, doling out punishments like an abusive parent. But this wasn't the God we believed in. We believed in a God who was goodness and mercy and love. How could one be *afraid* of such a God? Yet in today's readings, both the Old Testament reading and the gospel reading, we meet people who are completely terrified of God. And they are not terrified because God has been cruel, arbitrary, or violent to them. They are frightened because God has been good and merciful and loving to them.

The angel of the Lord comes to Gideon when he and his clan are in tough circumstances. The Midianites are stealing their food and destroying their crops and their herds, forcing the people of Gideon's tribe to hide out in caves and in the mountains so they could survive. Whenever they had food, they had to hide it, so the Midianites wouldn't take it from them. When the angel of the Lord appears to Gideon, Gideon basically says, "Well, where have you been all this time? Aren't you the great God who brought us out of Egypt? Aren't you supposed to be protecting us?" When God says: Go and save your people, Gideon says: But I'm too weak to do that, and besides, how do I know you will be with me? How do I know I can trust you? Show me a sign. Then I'll believe you. Through this whole dialogue, when he still believes that God is uncaring, neglectful, and cruel, Gideon is not afraid. He may be angry or hopeless, but not afraid. But when God shows him the sign he asks for, when God shows him that God is really with him, that God is faithful to him and loves him and will protect him, *then* Gideon is afraid—so terrified, in fact, he thinks he might die. The loving presence of God is far more frightening than God's long absence and the misery that went with it.

Jesus comes to Peter when Peter, too, is in tough circumstances. He's just come off a night of fishing during which he and his friends caught nothing. They are washing their nets when Jesus asks Peter to take him out on the water again. Probably that's the last thing he wants to do, or maybe the very last thing would have been to try any more fishing, which is the next thing Jesus asks him to do. As he's playing out the nets, perhaps he's feeling exhausted, hopeless, resentful—but not afraid. Nothing to be afraid of here. No, the fear comes when he feels the pull on the other end of the lines. The fear comes when he manages to wrestle the nets back into the boat and he sees the heaps and heaps of fish, sliding and cascading over the sides, till the boat is awash with them. *That* is terrifying. Exhaustion and hopelessness are nowhere near as frightening as this abundance, this outrageous gift, this love, this presence. It's too much: "Depart from me, Lord..." Peter pleads.

If Gideon and Peter are anything like us, it seems that my friends and I were wrong. We *can* be afraid of a God who is goodness and love. More than that, we can be afraid *of* God's goodness and love; somehow those are the aspects of God that are the most terrifying. God's grace, God's mercy, the abundance that God gives us, are far more scary than any cruelty or neglect would be. Our Presiding Bishop sends out a letter to all Episcopalians at Easter time (it's printed in the diocesan newsletter), and a few years ago he made the surprising observation that Easter was much more frightening than Good Friday. The horrors of the crucifixion, the cruelty and hatred manifest there, the worst that humans can do, all that is not as scary as what happens three days later. For in the resurrection the best that *God* can do is manifest: God's love, God's mercy, above all God's power to transform evil into good, to bring life out of death itself. Now *that's* scary. The women who found the empty tomb on Easter morning fled in terror. But why?

"I am a sinful man, O Lord." One reason why the love and goodness and abundance of God may frighten us is that, confronted with it, we feel so unworthy. In that dazzling light the darkness of our own lives stands out in sharp relief. I know how hard it can be for me to accept love from another human being, and there's that little voice in me that says, "If you really knew me, you couldn't possibly love me." I'm not good enough to be loved. If this is how we feel with human love, how much more intense it is when we are confronted with divine love. The poet George Herbert wrote a poem about the human soul meeting divine Love. The poem begins like this: "Love bade me welcome, yet my soul drew back, guilty of dust and sin. Yet quick eyed Love, observing me grow slack, drew nearer to me." And so the poem goes, with Love reaching out to the soul, and the soul keeps saying, "No, I can't come near you. I can't look at you. I'm not worthy of you." What you want to give me, God, I am not good enough to receive. I can't let you see me, can't let you know the parts of me that I am ashamed of. So depart from me, God, for I am a sinful person.

That sense of unworthiness might be one reason why God's love and abundance frighten us, so we want to push it away. But Gideon and Peter show us there's probably another reason too. For each of them, the gift of God's loving presence was a call to transform their lives. It was easy enough for Gideon, when he thought God had abandoned him, to convince himself that he couldn't do anything to help himself or his people. I'm too weak, my clan is too small, I can't do it. All I can do is hide out in caves and try to survive. It was easy enough for Peter to eke out his existence in the boats, catching just enough to survive. Sure it was miserable, but at least it was safe. It was what he knew. But when the love of God came into their lives, when they saw God's powerful grace, then they realized that there was a lot more to their lives than they had dreamed of before. The love of God, should they choose to accept it, was not going to leave them where it found them. It was a call to them to go out and do something they never would have thought they could do. It was going to draw them out into the deeps, into a life of risk, of passion, of being fully alive. Of being who God really created them to be.

Much of the time we live our lives only half alive. We get used to muddling along, just getting by, figuring that is all we can hope for, all we are good for. At least we are safe, in this stunted existence. But the astonishing love of God, should we choose to accept it, calls us out of this reduced existence into something much bigger and bolder and freer. The love of God calls us to do things we never thought we could do, to do great things for God's kingdom. God's power to transform promises to open our lives up to such richness and joy and challenge as is beyond our wildest dreams. It calls us to be who we truly are, to be fully and abundantly *alive*.

I have a friend who teaches art in a school for children who have "behavioral problems," and cannot be in the mainstream public schools. Most of her students are convinced they are failures. There was one student in her class who acted out this conviction more than the others. He was always late to class, never turned in his work, often cut class, and basically did everything he could to fail her course. Finally one day she pulled him aside, almost like a mother cat picking up a kitten by the scruff of his neck. She said to him, "Look, there's something you don't understand about my class. In my class, everyone is a success. Since you are in my class, you too are going to succeed. Now what are you going to do to get yourself in line with that reality?" It was as if she was saying to him: You are valuable. Now live that way. Be who you were created to be.

My friend offered to that child something like what Peter was offered in that boat. She offered this child the fundamental gift of telling him that he is valued. And from this gift she also offered this child a challenge. She said: Look, you are not meant to just muddle along and make do. You are meant to strive for excellence. You are meant to take risks, to learn how to do things you didn't think you could do. And you are meant to be an excellent human being as well, brave, kind, trustworthy. You are meant to be the person God created you to be, and then you are meant to pass these qualities on to others. She offered that child a taste of what God's gracious presence offers to us all.

Jesus stands before us always, even when we cannot sense his presence. His presence presents us with a choice, a choice that is always before us: to live our lives just to survive, to convince ourselves that we are failures and can only muddle along, to live out of our fears. Or to launch out into the depths, to accept the offer of transformation, to be called to a life of abundance beyond our wildest dreams. To accept the challenge of doing great things for the kingdom of God. To risk being who we really, truly are. This is the choice that is ever before us.

And if we cannot find the courage to choose life on our own, help is on the way. I said there were two images that stuck with me from the gospel story. But now there is a third: Jesus himself, standing in front of Peter, looking down at him, grave, tender, with perhaps a hint of a smile around the edges. And seeing Peter's fear, and also his longing to say yes, Jesus bends down, reaches out his hand to Peter and lifts him up. Jesus looks him straight in the eyes and says: "Do not be afraid. Follow me."

10

"Servant Leaders"

Frederick J. Streets

Now before the festival of the Passover, Jesus knew that his hour had come to depart from this world and go to the Father. Having loved his own who were in the world, he loved them to the end. The devil had already put it into the heart of Judas son of Simon Iscariot to betray him. And during supper Jesus, knowing that the Father had given all things into his hands, and that he had come from God and was going to God, got up from the table, took off his outer robe, and tied a towel around himself. Then he poured water into a basin and began to wash the disciples' feet and to wipe them with the towel that was tied around him. He came to Simon Peter, who said to him, "Lord, are you going to wash my feet?" Jesus answered, "You do not know now what I am doing, but later you will understand." Peter said to him, "You will never wash my feet." Jesus answered, "Unless I wash you, you have no share with me." Simon Peter said to him, "Lord, not my feet only but also my hands and my head!" Jesus said to him, "One who has bathed does not need to wash, except for the feet, but is entirely clean. And you are clean, though not all of you." For he knew who was to betray him; for this reason he said, "Not all of you are clean."

After he had washed their feet, had put on his robe, and had returned to the table, he said to them, "Do you know what I have done to you? You call me Teacher and Lord—and you are right, for that is what I am. So if I, your Lord and Teacher, have washed your feet, you also ought to wash one another's feet. For I have set you an example, that you also should do as I have done to you." (Jn. 13:1–15)

Those who feel called by God to do God's work in the world are humbled and frightened by this invitation from God. They wish to serve God fully with head and heart—to think and act on those things that please God and to have dwelling in them God's peace and joy. I would like for you to think about Jesus washing feet as an image of ministry found in the gospel of John. I will approach this story by telling you something about my own journey.

I attended the Lutheran church, which was next door to our home, from about the age of eight to eleven. There I committed to memory this ancient creed of the Christian church:

I believe in God, the Father almighty,
    creator of heaven and earth.
I believe in Jesus Christ, his only Son, our Lord.
He was conceived by the power of the Holy Spirit
    and born of the virgin Mary,
He suffered under Pontius Pilate, was crucified,
    died, and was buried.
He descended to the dead.
On the third day he rose again.
He ascended into heaven, and is seated at the right
    hand of the Father.
He will come again to judge the living and the dead.
I believe in the Holy Spirit,
the holy catholic church,
the communion of saints,
the forgiveness of sins,
the resurrection of the body, and the life everlasting.

Forty-one years ago, at the age of eleven, I responded to the minister's invitation to accept Jesus as my personal savior, was baptized and became a member of the church, not the Lutheran one next door; but, an African American Baptist church across town where my family had started attending. Three years after joining the Baptist church I felt called to the ministry, which meant to me then, preaching. This led to a tutorial process with the pastor to discern my call. Two years after this study began, I delivered my "trial sermon" to the congregation. I was sixteen years old. My high school was across the street from the church. I was a member of the concert and jazz bands, debate and football teams and the student council. I was known on the football team, not for my athletic ability but as "preacher Streets" because of the fervent prayers I said with the team before each game. God didn't always answer my prayer. I was well known in high school but I didn't feel popular. I think it had something to do with my going around announcing that I was going to be the first teenage Billy Graham. I looked rather nerdy and stern with my Austin Powers-like suit, minus the frilly shirt, and with a Bible under my arm. Nevertheless, on a Wednesday evening after football practice, I put on my suit, grabbed my Bible, and headed across the street to the church to preach my first sermon. My sermon title was taken from the story of Nehemiah's rebuilding the walls of Jerusalem: "I Am Doing a Great Work and I Can't Come Down."

They gathered at a midweek worship service held in the chapel of the church (not the main sanctuary) to hear the sermon and vote whether or not to institutionally sanction my sense of call.

The actions of examining a young person called to the ministry and confirming on him or her the title of licensed preacher or minister is a common practice among many Protestant evangelical churches and can be traced to the eighteenth century. A vote affirming my call to the ministry was taken after I preached, followed by a "love offering" and closing prayer. Each member extended to me their well wishes as they left the chapel on that cool October evening in 1966.

Two years later I entered college. The college experience expands our view of the world and ourselves. We are away from home and the watchful eyes of our parents. We do some stupid things while in college. It is a time of significant explorations, self-doubt, confusion, and personal growth. We may abandon some of what we were taught to believe and value. We do this in our effort to discover who we are, what we value and believe, and what we want to make of our lives. It is hoped that we get through college without making irrevocable mistakes and with a sense of satisfaction and self-understanding.

The summer of 1973, after completing my first year of divinity school, I returned to this church where I was "licensed to preach" to be examined and ordained as a minister of the church, as recommended to the congregation by a council created for this purpose.

I am amazed when I think back on those days by how much I thought I knew then about the ministry and journey of living the life of faith. The people who gathered to hear me proclaim the word of God in 1966 voted to support my call.

They did so not because they agreed totally with the content and theology of my sermon or were impressed by my preaching. No, they were affirming something else. They were supporting my desire and willingness to assume a formal role as a member of the clergy and applauded my intention to support the mission of the church. My understanding then of ordained ministry was limited to pastoring and preaching.

There are many ways we can use our gifts to live out in the world our sense of being called by God. However, it is neither the form of our Christian witness nor the formal roles of ministry we assume that I want you to think about today. These evolve over time and presuppose something else. The people who celebrated my call to the ministry by voting on my behalf cast their ballot in the hope and expectation that I would be a follower of Christ as much, if not more so, as I sought to be a leader in Christ's church as pastor and preacher.

Since my ordination I have studied many religious creeds and worshiped in a variety of Christian and non-Christian communities. A call to discipleship is an invitation to follow Christ. We do this by playing many roles to express our Christian witness in the church and beyond it. We support the church's mission as servants and followers of Christ.

Many people have negative associations with the idea of being a follower. Followers are like sheep. Docile and easily led, they lack autonomy and self-determination. Followers are stupid conformists who fail to succeed because they have no goals of their own. These negative images of what it means to be a follower prevent us from seeing its positive quality and essential dynamic relationship to being a leader.

In the story from John's gospel, Jesus demonstrated to his disciples the attitude and behavior of a servant leader. "[He] rose from supper and laid aside His garments, took a towel and girded Himself. After that, He poured water into a basin and began to wash the disciples' feet, and to wipe them with the towel with which He was girded" (Jn. 13:4–5, NKJV).

I will not offend your senses by discussing how unpleasant it can be to wash a person's feet. Imagine our beloved Savior waiting upon the feet of those who called him "Master"! Peter is the only one in the story who initially objects to this reversal of roles. Peter asked Jesus to wash him completely after Jesus told him that unless he washed his feet he could not be a part of him. Peter wanted to be part of what Jesus represented, but what this meant he only realized more fully later on.

Following Jesus meant for Peter and the other disciples discovering a new way of life, the meaning of which for them grew over time. We know that their relationship with Jesus was severely tested and the disciples' commitment was found wanting when they eventually betrayed, denied, and abandoned Jesus. This is not, however, the whole story of the relationship.

Jesus leads us by the life he lived, the death he died, and the resurrection he experienced. It is his whole life by which we are led to and have a relationship with God and one another. Jesus, as our leader, helps us to figure out right from wrong, good from evil, and to act according to what is right and good. Faith, love, and service become our attributes as followers of Jesus because these were the characteristics by which the Spirit of Jesus leads us to God. Servants of Christ help one another to have faith, to love, and to serve.

Our desire to follow Christ helps us create and sustain a church community with integrity. We define, shape, and nurture followers of Christ as members of his body: the church. We measure our success not by the world's standards but by whether we have used our variety of gifts as members of the body of Christ to help someone else.

Sometimes servants become leaders depending on the context, needs, and gifts they bring to a given situation. No matter which we are, leaders or followers, we are mutually called to be foot washers—or, if you prefer, servants of God. We are to care for one another as members of the body of Christ and serve the mission of the church in the broader community.

The demands on us as a servant-leader are at times formidable. We are called on, while anchored in a particular tradition and rooted by our faith, to minister to people with many different backgrounds, beliefs, and values. We need to be comfortable with ambiguity and pluralism in order to move with our witness of God within the complexity and beauty of the religious and cultural diversity of the people we are called on to serve. We need to cross many different boundaries as exemplars of community building. All of this and more is the work of ministry in a cultural context that is profoundly secular. Yet many people have a deep hunger to be part of something that is bigger than them, that gives their life meaning beyond material possessions or professional achievements. This is one reason for the spiritual awakening we see in many places. Jesus shows us by using a towel and bowl filled with water—by giving of himself—how this hunger is satisfied.

This work comes with a warning. We are not to be so heaven bound we are no earthly good; or so holy we cannot touch the dirt around us. We can be so filled with righteousness there is no room left in our hearts for the Holy Spirit—for grace.

To be a follower of Christ is counter to the culture's values of rugged individualism and self-centered capitalism. It is working with and on the behalf of others for the glory of God. We are sustained in this work by our own piety, the love our church community shares with us and by celebrating all the good things about our community and ourselves. It also requires, like all foot washing, that we see and touch the places where dirt has accumulated in order to clean them. This means we accept that we too have "dirty feet" in our own lives and community that need cleaning, and not just by our own hands but with the help of others. On some days we do the right thing and on other days we do the right thing for the right reason. We need the help of one another in our effort to keep our own feet clean as well as to clean the feet of others.

In the tale *A Father's Story*, by Andre Dubus, the character Father Paul says: "Belief is believing in God; faith is believing that God believes in you." Leaders and followers remind one another that God believes in them. This can make the difference between our feeling hope and feeling despair. God became flesh in Jesus Christ because God believed in us. God loved us to the point of suffering and dying on a cross because God believed in us. God held captivity captive and rose from death because God believed in us. And by God's grace, the power of our faith, and the presence of the Holy Spirit, God still believes in you and me! This gives us the capacity to love and serve others and help them to see and fulfill their potential.

The quality and movement of our lives are affected by the decisions we make. The choice I made to accept Christ forty years ago set in motion for me an ongoing process of discerning the meaning of following Christ while assuming many roles—chaplain, pastor, preacher, teacher, and social worker are a few. All of these roles are a means to an end.

The first song I sang in public as a member of the church choir has the lyrics "Lord, I want to be a Christian, in-a my heart." It is from the heart we serve, lead, follow, and ultimately find our way to God. Foot washing is not only an act but also an attitude. This is what the people of God were affirming years ago when I stood before them with all the audacity of my youthful faith in God. This is what we affirm in you. They commended me to God so that I too could learn what they knew about washing feet and so I commend to God those who wish to follow God with similar expectations and blessings. I must tell you in the words of my spiritual ancestors, "I wouldn't take nothing for my journey!" Would you? Amen.

Crisis

11

Getting to the Heart of the Matter

Peter Laarman

I don't think much of the way greatness is gauged and history is taught.

WILL CAMPBELL

In a society thoroughly infected with affluenza, we run the risk of becoming a people with everything and nothing. Our best-educated youth run a particular risk, for to them does the brass ring beckon most insistently. Despite the premise of liberal education that the best things in life are things money cannot buy—that the life well lived is itself the reward—our young women and men get a very different message if they are economically privileged and/or academically gifted. Their parents, their peers, their teachers, and their guidance counselors make it clear that in a culture where winners take all, it is a disgrace not to make it into the winners' circle. To be in the winners' circle means having a certain kind of income, an address ending in one of the magical ZIP codes, a sumptuous first home plus a second home in one of the preferred locations, and command of a shared set of references and tastes. It is tacitly understood that one's elite education will help supply these necessary references and tastes, but that that will be the extent of its usefulness.

It all forms a kind of grammar of faith. Only it's not Christian faith, which raises the question of what the person who is a pastor to such young people ought to be about. It will not suffice to urge them to be nice, because they already know how to be nice. Most of them will be looking to a minister for some alternative view, some counternarrative, unless they have already concluded that the chief function of the deity is to validate the entire existing arrangement. But such a presiding deity could only be one of the lifeless Baals and not the living God of Israel. It (for such a God would truly be an "it") could be little more than a fetish. And surely this campus minister, this very compelling and vibrant chaplain we like and respect, could not have been so stupid as to buy into a fraud.

I have long believed that ministers in campus settings enjoy a special privilege, for to them is entrusted the task of helping young adults begin to decode the spurious values of the dominant culture. Every faithful minister does this to a greater or lesser degree, but campus ministers do it with particular focus and intensity. Their capacity to do it well begins with the insight that the students gathered around them are indeed looking for an instruction and a nurturing that differ in kind from academic instruction and from the nurturing in the mores of the dominant culture that they have absorbed from infancy. Chaplains and campus ministers are privileged to be able to call the question of what it's all about—{all this questing and longing, all this joy and all this heartache that is the human journey. And they had better be ready with a good answer once the question has been called, because their youthful charges will be notoriously alert to any hint of evasion, any resort to empty piety, any withdrawal to a stance of elevated indifference to the urgency of the questioner's own life situation. *Most* of life amounts to a kind of extended crisis during adolescence and young adulthood, and no serious pastor will want to be found offering the children of America stones when they are asking for bread.

As Harry Adams's long and distinguished ministry illustrates so well, the task of preaching effectively to people in crisis and especially to young people in the throes of ethical discernment hinges on effective pastoral practice. One begins with a pastor's heart and with the deepest convictions of faith. One begins in the private conversation peculiar to the pastor's calling—in informal contact and in formal counseling—and then the same central insights and the same succor one offers privately find their public utterance in the pulpit. Thus, no matter what a sermon's title may be, the *real* subject is always how to live. The real subject is always "the subject": the individual human being in his or her striving.

And what are the core insights of faith that a good pastor first imparts in private? First, that life is broken in certain ways that cannot be fixed. Samuel Johnson wrote of the vanity of human wishes, but the psalmists and the teacher of Ecclesiastes got there first. We are cast into this world without a clue. The created world is beautiful, but the social world is complex and dangerous. What we can imagine for ourselves never seems to be what we achieve. We are subject to powerful sexual longings that confuse and torment us when they should be a source of pure delight. Our relationships are ambiguous: We let others down and are let down ourselves. The ones who love us best pass out of our lives, and sometimes they desert us. We have to work in order to live, but much of the work we do seems to be cut off from our deepest and best capacities. Anxiety, illness, injury, and death are never far from us, and the thought of our own eventual death makes no sense at all except as an unacceptable and outrageous fate—as the ultimate unfairness.

Life is broken and there is nothing we can do to fix it. Pastors know this. So do poets and playwrights. But pastors add a *nevertheless* to life's brokenness. *Nevertheless,* they insist, life is infinitely good and precious; *nevertheless,* they declare, "I will praise the Lord at all times: God's praise shall continually be in my mouth." No pastor can justify or defend this perspective to the student who comes to her in pain or in search of meaning. The pastor is a believer; for her, God's goodness and life's goodness are simply givens. They can't be demonstrated and they don't have to be shouted. They are visible in her eyes; they are heard in her tone of voice; they are expressed in her very carriage and manner. She would never deny life's tragic sense, for she herself feels it. But she also feels close connection with a very different story, with the divine comedy unfolding in an abiding love that envelops and transfigures our separate tragedies. Above her head, this pastor hears music in the air.

The pastor's everyday ministry of presence is grounded in the affirmation that nothing can separate her, and nothing can separate the person *before* her, from the love of God. She has found her own way to communicate this without having to preach it to the person she is counseling. And this core affirmation of faith supports and informs a further communication of wisdom about life's changes and the mutability of the human identity.

Students and young people have an especially hard time processing all the new information that pours in about themselves and their world during the sprint to adulthood. They objectify their parents—*really* objectify them!—for the first time, and they may not like what they see. Many come to a new political awareness that involves exchanging the notion of the United States as a good and virtuous nation for a much darker view of what this country is now and has always been about. And many who were raised in religious homes will reject or at least question the religious bromides of their childhood and wonder if their new, disenchanted worldview leaves any room at all for God.

This abrupt transition entails the shredding of so many old assumptions that it will sometimes seem as if there is nothing left for the student to call his own. "I was *that* person, and now I'm *this* person," he or she may feel, and such feelings are never without some related anxiety about who the *I* might be who experiences all of these changes.

The skilled pastor helps the young person come to see that the center of her identity is not given by her thoughts and assumptions about family, nation, or God. It is not what she *thinks* that yields her a secure identity but whether she can *feel* her original blessing as a child of God. The pastor's job in counseling always is to lead people to the heart of the matter, to open the pathway through which people can see and feel the most basic dimension of the life they are given, that most basic definition: child of God.

Child of God: That is who the student *is*, and that is who she *will* be, regardless of whether she trades in her family's Republican creed for radical socialism, regardless of whether she trains to be a banker instead of a teacher, regardless of whether she realizes during college that she is sexually attracted to women instead of men—even regardless of whether she has "lost her faith." She may be utterly confused and shaken by all of the changes she undergoes. Her pastor won't try to convince her that these changes aren't important—they are *very* important!—but will find a way to remind her that God's blessing still rests on her and that God may in fact be leading her to a richer, larger life—to the life she is meant to have—*through* these very tumultuous changes.

Preaching the Perspicuous Word

I have described the pastor's task at considerable length because of my contention that the preacher's success depends on a pastor's insights and a pastor's heart. What to say from the pulpit and even how to say it now becomes a fairly straightforward matter. Of course, the Spirit must finally give preaching its inward utterance. This is what is meant by Calvin's notion of a "perspicuous" Word that inwardly convinces the listener of its worthiness and truth even as it is being heard. Here the bread of life is not merely offered to the hungry mind and searching heart but is actually broken open and tasted.

Young people in transition or in crisis crave preaching that joins the macro and micro worlds in an affecting and convincing way. Such preaching illumines both axes of the Barthian vision: it evokes the grandeur and loftiness of God—God's freedom—even as it also evokes the *nearness* of the God who loves and calls us by name. Both are brought to life and made real. Neither works without the other, and young people in particular will reject the idea of intimate love if the *source* of such love is not properly identified.

Why would anyone care to hear a preacher tell her that God loves her if the God who is alleged to be doing the loving is a mere familiar spirit, some kind of aura, perhaps a psychological projection or ideation? In most New Age variants of divinity, God has been domesticated to the point that belief in divinity hardly seems worth bothering about.

In contrast to such dishwater, good preaching evokes God's surpassing glory in the course of evoking God's surpassing love. As in the most beautiful and best-loved psalms, in good preaching *wonder* and *reverence* arise from the realization that the Holy One who set the stars in their courses and established the boundaries of the sea, who created every living thing and filled the earth with beauty, who led the people out of bondage and who gave the life-giving Law from Sinai—that this selfsame God is also the God who made *me* and who redeems *my* life from destruction. It isn't necessary for the preacher to go on at length about God's glory—it can be brought out in something as simple and brief as the prefatory prayer—but the *sense* of it always has to be there.

Good preaching to people in crisis also takes the listener *inside* the Bible's world by projecting her right into the middle of the moral action. For the preacher this means choosing texts that really work to show what God is like when the chips are down, or that show how faithful people can discern God's presence and respond and stand fast in the midst of confusion and torment. Every preacher has some favorite texts that are fully alive with this kind of moral meaning; the challenge is to be able to eke it out of texts that may not be among the favored few in the repertoire. And always the preacher needs to go behind the outward action to uncover the moral disposition—the *inward* character—of the person or persons in the text whose behavior is being celebrated, because biblical narrative embeds and engraves all the moral meaning simply in what happens—without elaboration.

Here is where the strong preacher who is also an instinctive pastor will know how to make the most of all her informal contact with students along with her confidential counseling. The preacher must frame the theological context for the listening student: She must connect the God of glory to the God who calls each of us by name. But how will this theological reality be made real to the hearer? It becomes real by virtue of the way in which the preacher *herself* knows each student by name. The careful preacher here is not pretending to substitute for God, but neither should she hesitate *in this context* to preach and teach as God's representative. Just as she has already done in her conversation and counseling, the preacher standing in her pulpit *shows* the student what God is like: She shows it in her tone of voice and in the eye contact she now makes with her hearers.

Another way to make this point is to say that the effective preacher to a student congregation never fails to "show up" for her own sermon—she is fully present and her own life and deepest concerns are fully present—but she is careful at the same time not to grandstand and not to make the subject *her* story instead of *God's* story. She reserves her intensity and her passion for what the Word has to say; she is in the pulpit as the bearer of that Word and not as the bearer of personal anecdotes or personal opinions that may well interest and entertain the congregation but that can never feed them the bread of life.

Where Pastor and Prophet Meet

At the outset of this essay I suggested that it is the campus minister's special privilege to be able to help students decode the spurious values of the dominant culture. The sermon and not the private conversation is the principal vehicle for such decoding. It is in the pulpit that pastor and prophet meet. The effective campus minister accepts the responsibilities of the teaching elder and evokes in her preaching and teaching the world of what Walter Brueggemann calls the "prophetic imagination": an imagination that calls our ordinary "royal consciousness" into sharp question and that understands all the ways in which our society and economy ape pharaonic Egypt while yet pretending to be Israel.

Solid prophetic preaching on campus brings to bear its own pastoral dimension, because deconstructing the demonic and destructive character of the society can supply at least a *partial* key to some of the forces that threaten and trouble students individually. Vicious competition and grade-grubbing, abusive drinking, sexual violence, snobbery and social climbing, these campus realities don't fall from the sky; they are all rooted in a corrupted dominant culture that bears precious little resemblance to God's *shalom.* Christians believe that Christ as the bearer of *shalom* invites us not only to be healed individually but also, as Christ's body, to become active healers of the world's hurt. Prophetic preaching shapes and energizes this community of healers. The preacher's listeners are urged to see how doing justice and loving mercy means more than doing individual acts of kindness; it means engaging powers and principalities and dismantling the systems of injustice that authorize and perpetuate mass suffering throughout the world.

Rabbi Leo Baeck, a great sage and teacher, defined Jewish optimism as the settled inclination to "hold the world as it is in profoundest contempt." What distinguishes this outlook as optimism rather than mere cynicism is that it remains powerfully informed by an active and religiously grounded intention to *change* the unjust conditions one despises.

Today's campus preachers could do worse than imbue their students with a healthy dose of such Jewish optimism. The students already suspect that the world they inherit is not the best of all possible worlds. The faithful preacher points them toward a world that is—toward the already-but-not-yet reign of God, where righteousness and peace shall kiss.

12

"Of Wounds and Wonder"

Serene Jones

This sermon was delivered at the "Easter Rejoicing" worship service at Yale Divinity School's Marquand Chapel on April 23, 2001.

When it was evening on that day, the first day of the week, and the doors of the house where the disciples had met were locked for fear of the Jews, Jesus came and stood among them and said, "Peace be with you." After he said this, he showed them his hands and his side. Then the disciples rejoiced when they saw the Lord. Jesus said to them again, "Peace be with you. As the Father has sent me, so I send you." When he had said this, he breathed on them and said to them, "Receive the Holy Spirit. If you forgive the sins of any, they are forgiven them; if you retain the sins of any, they are retained."

But Thomas (who was called the Twin), one of the twelve, was not with them when Jesus came. So the other disciples told him, "We have seen the Lord." But he said to them, "Unless I see the mark of the nails in his hands, and put my finger in the mark of the nails and my hand in his side, I will not believe."

A week later his disciples were again in the house, and Thomas was with them. Although the doors were shut, Jesus came and stood among them and said, "Peace be with you." Then he said to Thomas, "Put your finger here and see my hands. Reach out your hand and put it in my side. Do not doubt but believe." Thomas answered him, "My Lord and my God!" Jesus said to him, "Have you believed because you have seen me? Blessed are those who have not seen and yet have come to believe."

Now Jesus did many other signs in the presence of his disciples, which are not written in this book. But these are written so that you may come to believe that Jesus is the Messiah, the Son of God, and that through believing you may have life in his name. (Jn. 20:19–31)

When Tony Hines asked me several months ago if I would preach for this Easter Rising service, the first thought I had—which of course came right out of my mouth—was a surprised, "You mean, I would have to preach on…resurrection? I don't know. I am really in more of a Good Friday kinda mode these days."

What Tony didn't know is that behind this rather strange response is that for the past year and a half, I have been doing work, as a systematic theologian, on traumatic violence and the cross. I have been struggling with the question: How does the crucifixion speak theologically to persons who have suffered events of overwhelming violence and who continue to be caught in the fractured psychic world such violence creates? As part of this project, I have spent days reading materials as diverse as narratives of the Holocaust and novels about sexual abuse, as well as cognitive psychologists' work on violence, brain function, and memory and even political theories on the future of a place like Rwanda, where a million people were killed in a hundred days.

In response to my (I assume) rather unexpected answer to his invitation, Tony looked only slightly perplexed and said kindly: "Wellllll, yes, I suppose you would have to say something about Easter in your sermon." And much to my own surprise and against my better judgment and all my inclination toward the cross, I said yes. So here you have before you this evening a "Good Friday Gal" struggling with resurrection.

My struggle has taken me on a rather unexpected journey into the lectionary text for this past Sunday, the story we just heard of the famous Doubting Thomas, the disciple who refused to believe that Jesus had been raised from the dead until he saw and touched the wounds in the crucified man's body. I am sure we have all heard the standard, now classic, modern sermon on Thomas, the sermon in which he is described as a kind of secular empiricist who won't believe without proof; the scientific mind who wants more evidence than provided by his friends' seemingly mythic stories; the cipher of modern, secular doubt. This is, at least, how I had come to understand the story: Thomas the scientific rationalist is finally converted by the sheer power of the truth.

But this time, when I came to the text bringing with me the weight of all these trauma stories, I met a very different Thomas and I heard the good news spoken to him in a very different way. Let us ask together, "What if we hear this as a story taking place in the midst of a community and a person who have suffered the profoundly fracturing force of violence and who are trying to make sense of what it means for the RESURRECTED SAVIOR to walk right into the middle of that space of psychic horror?"

To help us imagine this, let me say a few words about the cognitive literature that addresses what violence does to people's minds. The word *trauma* comes from the Greek word for "wound"—a word that doesn't actually appear in the text for today, but which has come to be associated with the holes made by the nails in Jesus' hands and feet—his wounds, his trauma. When cognitive psychologists use the term, it describes a particular kind of psychic wounding that occurs when—here's the classic definition—a person or a community experiences an event or events of overwhelming violence (perpetrated by human agents) that they perceive as threatening to annihilate them or another, against which they are powerless to resist, and that subsequently overwhelm their capacity to cope mentally. The wounds of this kind of violence are often felt not just in the moment of its occurrence, but through the establishment of cognitive patterns that can have long-term, devastating consequences.

Let me rehearse them for you briefly: In the moment of such violence the mind often shuts down; one cannot process the information coming in, and, consequently, reason draws a blank. One often has no conscious memory of such events, and yet in a haunting way the force of the events continues to circulate in one's imagination; intrusive reenactments constantly cut in. Survivors of traumatic violence are often described as living in a state of "not being present"—the self fractures off from itself, either feeling from a distance or feeling nothing at all. And this reaction of shutting down is particularly acute when an incident of violence is not named as such by the community. No part of the victim's life remains untouched by this fracturing, although for many, there continues to be a high level of social functioning.

For me, no one captures this reality better than that famous poet of trauma, Emily Dickinson. Hear the words she uses to describe how violence can rupture reason and devastate our capacity to know.

> I felt a Funeral, in my Brain,
> And Mourners to and fro
> Kept treading—treading—till it seemed
> That Sense was breaking through—
> And when they all were seated,
> A Service, like a Drum—
> Kept beating—beating—till I thought
> My Mind was going numb—
> And then I heard them lift a Box
> And creak across my Soul
> With those same Boots of Lead, again,
> Then Space—began to toll,
> As all the Heavens were a Bell,
> And Being, but an Ear,
> And I, and Silence, some strange Race
> Wrecked, solitary, here—
> And then a Plank in Reason, broke,
> And I dropped down, and down—
> And hit a World, at every plunge,
> And Finished knowing—then—[1]

With Midrashic boldness, let us look again at Thomas's story and, in light of Dickinson's imagery, ask: Did Thomas "feel a funeral in his brain"? Had, perhaps, a Plank in his Reason broken? Had the horror of his leader's tortured death and his own vulnerability to violence "finished his knowing"? Perhaps his

---

[1]Emily Dickinson, *The Complete Poems of Emily Dickinson* (Boston: Little Brown, 1924), Poem 280, written in 1861.

doubt is not that of the robust empiricist but rather that of the undone, fractured victim who, in a sense, cannot know. Perhaps Thomas is the person in these stories of resurrection who bears for us the collective weight of all the trauma survivors of history who doubts because the very activity of their knowing has been violently, violently rent asunder.

Karl Barth, of all people, helps us to read this story in this manner. The story tells us that when Jesus first comes, Thomas is not "with them." He is, quite simply, "absent." Is Thomas the figure of all those many victims of violence who are just "not there"—perhaps present in body but not in mind—when Jesus first shows up? How many times have I stood at a pulpit to preach the good news and looked out to see before me the bodies of parishioners who I know "are not there"—the harms of their lives rendering them blank?

Barth further reminds us that in John's telling of this resurrection event, even when Thomas is finally there, with his friends, "the doors were locked." With Thomas himself closed in behind these doors, the entryway leading into his imagination has also been slammed shut. And for good reason: He (and his friends) feared being preyed upon. Here, I can tell you (as perhaps we all can) of those times when it is not arrogance but the devastating legacy of inflicted cruelties that closes our minds.

So, here we have Thomas doubting…doubting that Christ has been raised, doubting that the one he knew had been executed was with them. And this brings me to that time in the sermon when I am supposed to do what I told Tony I dread doing: I am supposed to talk about resurrection.

I must be honest with you: Having reached this place in the story, I find myself still not knowing what to say—my voice falters, reason stops…

But here's the difference: Formed in the space of this amazing story, this "not knowing" is not the halting voice of a reason broken by violence; it is the not knowing that stands with wonder in the space of unimaginable hope. And this hope resides not in gazing at Thomas, but in shifting our gaze to Jesus. What do we see when we look there? Let me describe three things.

First, Jesus walks through the closed doors: We don't have to open them, or even be able to open them. Further, Jesus invites Thomas to touch his wounds before Thomas even has the chance to ask. The grace of the resurrection is sheer, unimaginable gift: It is not generated out of the psychic space created by our traumas. And we don't have to figure out evil or pierce through the cognitive nightmares of trauma in order to be greeted by grace. Jesus walks through the locked doors, stands in the space of Thomas's terror, and is simply, physically, irreducibly there.

Second, the hope that encounters us in Jesus may be unfathomable but it is not empty of content. What does Jesus say when the disciples see him? What are the words that mark his presence, his linguistic body? Peace be with you. The promise of the resurrection is a promise of peace, a promise of life, a promise deeply just and abundant with mercy. It is safe and whole and good.

And finally (and perhaps most importantly for the Thomases of our world, the traumatized Thomas in all of us who survives the daily violence of our culture), when we imagine this previously unimaginable peace, this gift, we will do so only as we touch the wounds of crucifixion. We know the risen Christ only insofar as we know the tortured, murdered Christ. And when we meet Christ and proclaim with Thomas, "*my Lord and my God*," we come to Emily Dickinson's "funeral-finished reason" and, standing there, we will not try to look around it, over it, under it, or simply ignore it—we will look through it. The stories of our hopes will only be as strong as our capacity to name that which our hopes contradict.

Is this all we can say about resurrection? I don't know. But at this point, I am wont to defer to the poets among us because they are usually much more adept than theologians in helping us to imagine the unimaginable—the space born of wounds and wonder. And poets, when they're good, take us to this place in a breathy language that is strong enough to touch wounds and heal us while also being open enough to invite us into the world of grace, ever anew.

So, I leave you with this: An image that comes to us from another great writer, Toni Morrison, who in *Jazz* invokes for us a grace-filled space where the doors are not locked because violence no longer threatens, where the cognitive shutdown of trauma itself becomes unimaginable. She gives us, in detailed corporeality, a glimpse of what a community, formed in the body of the wounded, resurrected Christ might look like to those whose doubt is born of trauma.

I want to inhabit, walk around a site where the race is both spoken and rendered impotent, a place already made for me, both snug and wide open....A place of a kind of "out-of-doors safety" where "a sleepless woman could always rise from her bed, wrap a shawl around her shoulders and sit on the steps in the moonlight. And if she felt like it, she could walk out of the yard and on down the road. No lamp and no fear. A hiss-crackle from the side of the road would never scare her because whatever it was that made that sound, it wasn't something creeping up on her. Nothing for miles around thought she was prey. She could stroll as slowly as she liked, thinking of food preparations, of family things, or lift her eyes to the stars and think of war or nothing at all. Lampless and without fear she could make her way.

And if a light shone from a window up a ways and the cry of a colicky baby caught her attention, she might step over to the house and call out softly to the woman inside trying to soothe the baby. The two of them might take turns massaging the infant's stomach, rocking, or trying to get a little soda water down. When the baby quieted they could sit together for a spell, gossiping, chuckling low so as not to wake anybody else. The woman could go back to her bed then, refreshed and ready to sleep, or she might stay her direction and walk further down the road—on out, beyond, because nothing around or beyond considers her prey.[2]

A wild fantasy?

Jesus said to Thomas, "Have you believed because you have seen me? Blessed are those who have not seen and yet have come to believe." And as John concludes, "These things, brothers and sisters, are written so that you might come to believe that Jesus is the Messiah, the Son of God, and that through believing you have life in his name...the wounded one, the risen one."

---

[2]Toni Morrison, "The House that Race Built," *Jazz* (New York: Knopf, 1992), 9–10.

13

"Stay in Jerusalem"

Richard E. Spalding

This sermon was delivered at The Church of the Covenant in Boston on the seventh Sunday in Eastertide, 1999.

In the first book, Theophilus, I wrote about all that Jesus did and taught from the beginning until the day when he was taken up to heaven, after giving instructions through the Holy Spirit to the apostles whom he had chosen. After his suffering he presented himself alive to them by many convincing proofs, appearing to them during forty days and speaking about the kingdom of God. While staying with them, he ordered them not to leave Jerusalem, but to wait there for the promise of the Father. "This," he said, "is what you have heard from me; for John baptized with water, but you will be baptized with the Holy Spirit not many days from now."

So when they had come together, they asked him, "Lord, is this the time when you will restore the kingdom to

Israel?" He replied, "It is not for you to know the times or periods that the Father has set by his own authority. But you will receive power when the Holy Spirit has come upon you; and you will be my witnesses in Jerusalem, in all Judea and Samaria, and to the ends of the earth." When he had said this, as they were watching, he was lifted up, and a cloud took him out of their sight. While he was going and they were gazing up toward heaven, suddenly two men in white robes stood by them. They said, "Men of Galilee, why do you stand looking up toward heaven? This Jesus, who has been taken up from you into heaven, will come in the same way as you saw him go into heaven."

Then they returned to Jerusalem from the mount called Olivet, which is near Jerusalem, a sabbath day's journey away. When they had entered the city, they went to the room upstairs where they were staying, Peter, and John, and James, and Andrew, Philip and Thomas, Bartholomew and Matthew, James son of Alphaeus, and Simon the Zealot, and Judas son of James. All these were constantly devoting themselves to prayer, together with certain women, including Mary the mother of Jesus, as well as his brothers. (Acts 1:1–14)

"While he was blessing them, he withdrew from them…" (Lk. 24:51)

That's how Luke describes the final moment of leave-taking between the risen Christ and the disciples in the last verses of his gospel—to which this morning's reading of the ascension story in the first chapter of Acts begins the sequel. Luke is the only gospel writer brave or whimsical enough to include in his story the tender moment of contradiction, when Jesus left the disciples on their own: "and as he blessed them he withdrew from them."

So much of the religious life links unthinkable opposites like that, in such a matter-of-fact way that at first you don't notice how outrageous the juxtaposition really is. The beloved prayer of Francis of Assisi strings all those paradoxes together: It is in giving that we receive, in pardoning that we are pardoned, in mortality that we discover life…In Jesus (the suffering servant, the wounded healer, the humiliated messiah), God distilled the essential paradoxes of this human existence out of the improbable alchemy of flesh and spirit—and then Jesus gave it all away, lost his life so that we could find it. And at the very final instant of their togetherness, so the story goes, of all the things he could have been doing at the last moment they ever saw him, he was blessing them; of all the things that could have been happening as he blessed them, he left them. Even while he made himself absent from the face of this world, he instilled his presence among them; and when he left them most alone, they began to understand what it would mean to be together.

And, according to Luke, Jesus' last explicit instruction to them was every bit as paradoxical as so many of his gestures, his words, his presence. Remain in Jerusalem, he said. To them, and maybe to us, this last teaching they heard from his lips might at first sound appropriately pious: Stay where religious things happen, near the temple, at the destination of pilgrimage. Luke actually calls it not a teaching, but an order—and when you think about it, that's probably what it would have had to be. Maybe the disciples didn't realize it at first, as they gazed up into heaven; maybe (in the paradox of these things) they needed to have their reverie grounded by angelic voices at their elbows. But even in the midst of blessing and leaving them, their master of paradox was bidding them return to the place from which, perhaps more than any other place, they must by that time have longed to be freed forever.

Jerusalem, Jerusalem. He had wept over it himself. "City that kills the prophets and stones those who are sent to it! How often have I desired to gather your children together as a hen gathers her brood under her wings, and you were not willing" (Lk. 13:34). Now the brooding maternal protection seemed to have flown once and for all—and he sent them wingless back into the city that could turn in an instant on a hinge of anger, and shout for him, or any of them, to endure public torture.

From the little hill they call the Mount of Olives just to the east, you can see the whole city spread out before you. And as they looked back that day, the skyline must have ached with echoes, a panorama of all the places in which he'd been with them in that charged week barely a month before: the Beautiful Gate through which he rode, the temple court where he turned the tables on the religious establishment, the house with the upper room where they'd eaten the Passover together, the Praetorium of his sham trial, the Via Dolorosa he'd walked from there, dragging his cross to the hill in the stone quarry where it had seemed that everything had ended, and the empty cave where they had received the surprise of their lives. Go back into all of that and wait, he instructed. How much this landscape must have made the Galileans ache to simply limp back home to places they understood, places that didn't threaten their lives, to ponder the thousand questions that the resurrection had left with them over a quiet life of fishing. But: remain in the city, he said—and then, while blessing them, he left them. Stay in Jerusalem.

No one tells this story except Luke—which might make you wonder about whether it's true or not...except that it's so very like Jesus, on behalf of God, to ask you, even while blessing you, to do the thing that is the most unimaginable. "Stay in Jerusalem..." reminds you of other instructions that feel like facing into the full force of a hurricane—words like "you therefore must be perfect," or "you lack one thing: go and sell what you have and give to the poor..." or "unless you become like children..." or "stay awake with me just one hour."

They returned. They left the mountain and risked the streets again. They went first, Luke says, "to the room upstairs where they were staying," and though he doesn't say it explicitly, it seems to me that it has to have been the upper room in which they broke Passover bread together—the room in which Thomas held out for actually seeing the nail holes in the resurrected hands and the room in which Jesus held out those hands, caught Thomas's resurrected faith and hurled it into history. Luke goes around the room and names them, one by one, the ones who stayed: Peter and John, James and Andrew...together with certain women (evidently so much more important to us than they were to Luke), including Mary...They were praying constantly, Luke says, but Luke delicately avoids saying much about the conditions that made constant prayer essential: surrounded by danger, and drenched in memories, and bereft of organization, and utterly at the mercy of the future. They stayed in Jerusalem, in a room upstairs, waiting for something they'd never seen, and couldn't be sure they'd even recognize when it came—stayed because they loved and trusted so much the one who sent them back.

You know that room. You've been there, I'm almost certain. It is the place you stay, not because you want to, but partly because you want not to. The place you stay because you are called by your name there. The place you stay because the thing that might happen there—if you recognize it when it comes—might make all the difference, might banish finally and forever the fear that breathes on all sides around you, might answer the questions with which you ache, might give you a way to organize your understanding of what your work really is, might make clear the way into the looming future. The place you stay because of the kind of love that's not so much about what you want to do as it is about what you have to do.

Stay in the city. Stay, not because of what the schools are, but because of what they might be; not because of the current administration but because of the next one. Stay in the city, not because the battles for equality and justice have been won, but because here is a place where you can see that they haven't been won. Take to its streets at least once a year, just as a personal spiritual discipline, when your day of pride comes around, or when the day comes to carry the torch for others whose hunger, or illness, or fear keeps them from walking. Stay where it exhausts you to think of re-engaging the struggle, so that the struggle itself is not exhausted.

Stay in the church. Stay, not because of what the church is, but because of what it might be. Pour out your weariness or disillusionment or your doubts there—not because it is always the most satisfying thing to do, or the tidiest, but because it's in service to the most meaningful things to do—and because pouring them out is better than holding them in. Stay Presbyterian: Stay in the room where fear breathes audibly—stay not because you can be sure you'll ever vanquish the fear and win for yourself a real place at the table, but because you can't get up from the table anymore without leaving a piece of yourself there; stay to show them that. Stay UCC: Stay in the tempting room where things seem better but aren't necessarily yet. Stay in the threadbare old neo-Gothic building: stay with the scarred plaster and linoleum and stay even in the inadequate light because sometimes you can almost believe there will be more light. Stay with the headache of always trying to do so much, so much, and stay in the midst of the din of faith that's trying to soar with barely enough room to spread its wings to their full span.

Stay in Central America—stay with the village that has no topsoil left, after the hurricane—no crops or animals left, after the hunger—no money left, after the triumph of other people's "free markets." Stay, not because the need will ever stop, but because the need will never stop mattering; stay because the need will never stop teaching you things you just have to know. Stay as a way of believing that the suffering of a small community of campesinos has a place in the heart of God. Stay as a way of finding the heart of God in your own heart.

Stay in the family, if you can; stay unless and until it becomes a place of death to you. There are almost always more ways of staying than you probably realize, and though some of them will cost more than your spirit can pay, other ways will be more possible than you can see now. Stay in relationship as long as you can, because though it's not the easiest thing to do, it's easier than lugging the unreconciled bitterness around with you wherever else you go. And when you have to leave, then pray for the wholeness of the people who grieve you and who aggrieve you, the people you leave behind and the ones who leave you behind, and pray for a wholeness of the family we have not yet imagined. Pray for the peace of Jerusalem.

Stay in Jerusalem. It is a landscape with many rooms, places you've been and places you long to be and places you hope never to be again. The room of indignities suffered is there, and maybe a day will come for you to return to that room and discover your dignity unscathed after all. The room of grief is there, and you will be surprised how even tears can finally help make a home— for blessing and parting, parting and blessing are not as contradictory as they seem at first. The room of anger is there, and sooner or later will insist that you call there, to leave something behind you've been carrying for so long you've stopped noticing its astonishing weight. And the room of memory is there—the place where you'll recollect all the places you've been that God has been with you, all the addresses that have been made temples because God has visited you there.

So many rooms—all upper rooms when you go back to them: rooms with a view. In the house of our following God there are indeed many mansions. Each of them is a place known to the heart of Jesus—in which our suffering is known to him, or our joy, or our floundering in the contradictions and paradoxes. Remain there, he says—because that is where the promise will be fulfilled. Jerusalem, precisely because it is the place where the struggle is engaged the most deeply, and with the highest stakes, is the place where the gift will be given. Jerusalem, precisely because it is the place in which it is the hardest to breathe around the hurt and uncertainty and memory and need, is the place where the breath of spirit will inspire, because it is the capital of paradox. Go back there, wingless and alone, and wait for the promise of breath to lift you to soaring after all, to a new way of being together, and a new way of seeing. When you get there, maybe go around the room and say the names—because they'll help you to stay. Go around the room, and say the name of the one you love and trust who sent you here on a wing and a promise.

14

"Going Home"

David L. Bartlett

This sermon was delivered on the 2001 Parents' Weekend at Lynchburg College.

Then Jesus said, "There was a man who had two sons. The younger of them said to his father, 'Father, give me the share of the property that will belong to me.' So he divided his property between them. A few days later the younger son gathered all he had and traveled to a distant country, and there he squandered his property in dissolute living. When he had spent everything, a severe famine took place throughout that country, and he began to be in need. So he went and hired himself out to one of the citizens of that country, who sent him to his fields to feed the pigs. He would gladly have filled himself with the pods that the pigs were eating; and no one gave him anything. But when he came to himself he said, 'How many of my father's hired hands have bread enough and to spare, but here I am dying of hunger! I will get up and go to my father, and I will say to him, "Father, I have sinned against heaven and before you; I am no longer worthy to be called your son; treat me like one of your hired hands."' So he set off and went to his father. But while he was still far off, his father saw him and was filled with compassion; he ran and put his arms around him and kissed him. Then the son said to him, 'Father, I have sinned against heaven and before you; I am no longer worthy to be called your son.' But the father said to his slaves, 'Quickly, bring out a robe—the best one—and put it on him; put a ring on his finger and sandals on his feet. And get the fatted calf and kill it, and let us eat and celebrate; for this son of mine was dead and is alive again; he was lost and is found!' And they began to celebrate.

"Now his elder son was in the field; and when he came and approached the house, he heard music and dancing. He called one of the slaves and asked what was going on. He replied, 'Your brother has come, and your father has killed the fatted calf, because he has got him back safe and sound.' Then he became angry and refused to go in. His father came out and began to plead with him. But he answered his father, 'Listen! For all these years I have been working like a slave for you, and I have never disobeyed your command; yet you have never given me even a young goat so that I might celebrate with my friends. But when this son of yours came back, who has devoured your property with prostitutes, you killed the fatted calf for him!' Then the father said to him, 'Son, you are always with me, and all that is mine is yours. But we had to celebrate and rejoice, because this brother of yours was dead and has come to life; he was lost and has been found.'" (Lk. 15:11–32)

Here's one picture I will always carry from September 11.

It's a story on the local news station, a young man from a town in Connecticut just down the road. The young man has just arrived at the train station, on his way home from the World Trade Center where he worked. He's telling the horrible story of what he has seen in a city that used to be familiar but that turned in an instant into a far and terrifying country. And his father, who came from home to meet him at the station, is hurrying along behind him, walking faster than a man that age ought to walk and breathing harder than he ought to breathe. And every twenty seconds or so the young man interrupts his awful dialogue and looks back and says: "Are you all right, Dad?"

And then again: "Are you all right, Dad?" And then to the reporters: "That's enough now; we just want to go home."

At the end of Jesus' famous parable the aging father comes running down the steps as fast as his legs will carry him and faster than his heart should bear, dashes down the road to welcome his son whom he thought was lost in his own domestic tragedy, and if the son has any sense at all, when he's through giving his little repentance speech he'll say what he ought to say: "Are you all right, Dad?"

And then father and son together do what parents and children always want to do when crisis strikes and pain overwhelms. They embrace each other and head for home.

Look, on that awful Tuesday every parent knew in the gut what we know in the back of our minds—that life is fragile, that even Manhattan, which is just down the road from my house and even Arlington, which may be just down the road from yours— can become the far country. We called our sons. Students at the school where I teach pulled out their cell phones or hurried to the pay phones to call their children and to call their parents. Everybody who could headed home; everybody else wished they could be home with each other.

Here's what we remembered on Tuesday, September 11, 2001…That even if we live to be a hundred and our children live to be a hundred and ten, that life is short and our time together is shorter.

That sometimes we all need to come home, and if we can't get home to the same house at least we need to get home to one another.

And our story gives us some clues about how to come home to one another. The story we call the prodigal son is really a story about coming home. A son who's gone a long way from home and wants to come back. A son who's just over on the back forty and can't decide whether to come back. A father who's ready to rejoice in a homecoming.

The story, like all of Jesus' parables, is about at least two things. It's a story about God's love for God's family, and we'll come back to that; but it's also a story about how life might look in a family that tries faithfully to make a home for one another. It gives us some clues to how we might make home for one another in these difficult times—even when we have to do it long distance.

Here's a word for parents. What strikes me about this story is how well the father respects the individuality of his children, their dignity and freedom if you will.

He doesn't try to make his children over into his own image. He knows that one is a freer spirit than he is, and the other is a little stuffier. But he doesn't try to make them over into himself.

And he treats each of the children in ways that respect their differences from one another—but always with respect and love. We all remember from the story that the father runs down the road to greet the prodigal; but we forget that he heads down the road to reach the older brother too.

To the prodigal he says: "Welcome home." To the older brother he says: "Son, you are always with me, and all that I am is yours."

Different words for different people, but the same deep, respectful, love.

Years ago my grandmother died. She had five children and eighteen grandchildren. There was a moving funeral service, and then a luncheon at the church, and as we sat around remembering her what struck me was that my grandmother had made every one of her children and grandchildren feel as if she or he were the most special person in the world. Highly educated and not very educated; pretty well-to-do and pretty poor; those who worked night and day and those who spent most of their time partying—everyone loved and respected for the person they were.

About eight years ago Mr. Rogers, who had just retired from PBS, came to Yale to give a lecture. He was lecturing in a big auditorium, and as the time came for the lecture hundreds of graduate students and faculty arrived at the auditorium bringing their children to see Mr. Rogers. But there was no room, because for an hour the auditorium had been full of undergraduates—undergraduates who, like all college students, spent a lot of their time feeling pressure to succeed and to be who their teachers and their parents wanted them to be.

They came to see Mr. Rogers because not that many years ago they had sat in front of the TV, and he had looked them in the eye and said what every person needs to hear: "I like you just the way you are."

You know how he made them feel: He made them feel at home.

There's a word here for children too. Jesus' story really acts out Moses' commandment. "Honor your father and mother." Not like them all the time; that's too much to ask. Not agree with them all the time: how boring that would be. But *honor* them. Grant them the benefit of the doubt: Admit that they're human too, and cherish their right to be human.

At the beginning of the story, when the prodigal son comes to his father and says: "Give me my share of your estate," he's really saying: "Listen, I'm not willing to wait for you to die to give me what's coming in your will, so I'll just treat you as dead. Hand it over."

Toward the end of the story when he comes heading down the road he's thinking: "Father, I have sinned against heaven and before you." Whatever else that means, it means now I know that you're a person too. And I have come to give you the honor you deserve.

Hallmark has gotten rich on Mother's Day and Father's Day, and those holidays do no harm. But we'd do better if we thought of every day as Human Being Day. Treat your mother and your father as human beings.

Make them feel at home.

And a word for all of us in families. In a family you keep forgiving: There is no shelf date on forgiveness, no time when it's out of fashion or out of date or out of place.

The younger son comes down the road practicing his speech of repentance: "I have sinned against heaven and before you. I am no longer worthy to be called your son," but before he can even get the words out of his mouth, he sees his father running down the road, to greet him, invite him to a party, welcome him home.

The older son, understandably peeved, stands in the field and says to his father, "Why are you throwing a party for this son of yours?" And the father hears that business about "your son" and makes the point: "Your brother; it's your brother; back from the far country. Forgive him; come to the party; come home."

Look, you know how it goes, in every family every one of us is wronged and does wrong; every one of us gets hurt and hurts the other. What holds it together is forgiveness.

Two weeks ago today my Uncle Fred, Jonah's great Uncle Fred, died after a long and good life. Years ago when I was a child and our family was visiting Fred and Polly and their family, we had a big day planned. We were going to the zoo. But before we could go to the zoo, Uncle Fred, who was an excellent handyman, wanted to lay the cement for a new sidewalk at his home.

I appointed myself Guardian of the Cement, and as my brothers and sisters and cousins milled around, I marched back and forth by the sidewalk proclaiming, "Don't step in the cement, or we can't go to the zoo." Forth I marched and announced and then back; forth, and then back—of course right into the wet cement.

The story of family life; declaring one thing with our lips and doing something else with our feet. Devastated, I ran to our family car to hide in the back seat, till Uncle Fred came out to find me, forgive me. Assure me we could still go to the zoo.

Welcome me home. No family without forgiveness; with forgiveness, family, celebration, home.

Of course when the prodigal comes home, and we hope when the older brother comes in from the field, the father and the anonymous mother and the sons will do what you need to do to make family family, to make home home: They share a meal.

A couple of years ago I was asked to speak to some church groups about how we could strengthen our relationships with our children, and my spouse shared with me some striking research. The sociologists had done a study of adolescents using a very simple distinction. One group of young people had been in trouble with the law, and the other had not.

And the sociologists wanted to know if there was anything different about the families of the two groups of people. They found one surprising distinction: it wasn't a distinction of how wealthy one group was, or how educated, or how religious.

It was this: The young people who were not in trouble were much more likely to come from families where at least once a day everyone sat down together to a meal.

Think about it. Of course it wasn't just the food. It was the time: time for each other, respect for each other, gratitude for the gifts of bounty and the gifts of family. It was taking time in the midst of all our busyness to make house home.

Every family needs its meals together; and the human family too. We are about to come to a table for a meal prepared by a loving father who sent his son into a very far country.

And before he was arrested and killed, and raised from the dead, Jesus set a table for his brothers and sisters, older and younger, prodigal and proper; all were welcome to his meal.

This is a feast of love prepared for all God's children, and when we come to this table, we declare that we are God's family and sisters and brothers to one another.

When we come to this table, wherever it is set and however far we've come, we come to the place where we belong and we come with the people we belong to.

Welcome home.

15

"God Bless America"

William Sloane Coffin

This sermon was delivered at the United Church of Strafford (UCC) in Strafford, Vermont, on October 14, 2001.

> Though the fig tree does not blossom,
> and no fruit is on the vines;
> though the produce of the olive fails
> and the fields yield no food;
> though the flock is cut off from the fold
> and there is no herd in the stalls,
> yet I will rejoice in the Lord;
> I will exult in the God of my salvation. (Hab. 3:17–18)

"You have heard that it was said, 'An eye for an eye and a tooth for a tooth.' But I say to you, Do not resist an evildoer. But if anyone strikes you on the right cheek, turn the other also; and if anyone wants to sue you and take your coat, give your cloak as well; and if anyone forces you to go one mile, go also the second mile. Give to everyone who begs from you, and do not refuse anyone who wants to borrow from you.

"You have heard that it was said, 'You shall love your neighbor and hate your enemy.' But I say to you, Love your enemies and pray for those who persecute you, so that you may be children of your Father in heaven; for he makes his sun rise on the evil and on the good, and sends rain on the righteous and on the unrighteous. For if you love those who love you, what reward do you have? Do not even the tax collectors do the same? And if you greet only your brothers and sisters, what more are you doing than others? Do not even the Gentiles do the same? Be perfect, therefore, as your heavenly Father is perfect. (Mt. 5:38–48)

I've always aspired to be both tough-minded and tenderhearted. It strikes me as the Christian thing to be. "Make love your aim," says Paul, and doesn't love demand the utmost in clear-sightedness?

With this aspiration in mind, I approach my nonbiblical text for today's sermon. It is the title of Irving Berlin's song "God Bless America."

During the recent weeks of grief and anguish and the civic passion that rose from the smoking debris, I would have liked to have sung Woody Guthrie's more inclusive, "This land is your land, this land is my land," with its specific mention of New York. But Americans clearly wanted to sing "God Bless America," and I joined in, even more eagerly when we sang "America the Beautiful," which I have long held should be our national anthem.

"God Bless America." Every one of these three words begs for interpretation, and I can only give you mine and eagerly await yours.

When you grow older, you can get along with less, even fewer biblical stories and sayings. But I could never survive without 1 John 4:16b, "God is love and they who abide in love abide in God and God abides in them." To me, two convictions about God's love are absolutely fundamental: (1) God's love is poured out equally on all of God's children from the pope to the loneliest wino on the planet; (2) God's love doesn't seek value, it creates it. It is not because we have value that we are loved, but because we are loved that we have value. In short, our value is a gift, not an achievement.

In God's sight we are all equal and equally important. So I guess the first reason Christ commands us to love our enemies is because God loves them. And notice that the very same sentence in which Christ commands us to love our enemies, goes on: "For God makes his sun to rise on the evil and on the good, and sends rain on the just and the unjust." In Reinhold Niebuhr's commentary, "A non-moral nature is made the symbol of God's transmoral mercy."

In church we are always singing about "a wideness in God's mercy," of "one great fellowship divine throughout the whole wide earth," about how "other lands have sunlight too, and clover, and skies are everywhere as blue as mine." In all these hymns we are affirming God's same impartial love for all people with no special privileges in it for only some. In other words, "God Bless America" means "God bless Afghanistan" too, not to mention Iraq and North Korea.

It may be impossible to believe for the Taliban and hard to believe for some Americans, but there is no special Providence for any nation at the expense of any others. To lobby in the courts of the Almighty for special favors is a waste of time.

Moreover, there is no simple correlation of reward for good people and nations and punishment for evil people and nations. That's the point of the book of Job, isn't it? And on Calvary there are the three crosses, two for criminals who couldn't meet the standards of the law, and one for the Savior who rose so far above them. That's life. God provides minimal protection but maximum support.

But God's love doesn't necessarily mean approval. Far from it. God hates hateful things. God doesn't love carnage. In the wake of the attacks on September 11, a host of Muslims, Shiite and Sunni, loudly condemned the terrorism as strictly forbidden in Islamic law. Terrorists in Islam, as in Christianity, are heretics. But just as God didn't applaud the demented sophistication of the hijackers' crimes, so God was not able to prevent the thousands of gruesome deaths they caused. And they were heart wrenching. But if God is love, then human freedom is for real. Freedom may be a burden, and choice scary. But freedom is the precondition of love. We are not slaves but children of our Father, free to do good, free to sin. Let's be tough-minded: When in anguish over any human violence done any innocent people, we ask of God, "How could you let that happen?" let's remind ourselves that God is asking that same question of us.

God doesn't go around the world with fingers on triggers, fists around knives, hands on the control of airplanes. It is understandable that in moments of grief we feel God's absence. The reality of grief is the solitude of pain—"My God, my God, why hast thou forsaken me?" But Psalm 22 only begins that way; it ends with the reaffirmation that God does not hide God's face from the afflictions of the afflicted. Therefore let our consolation rest in the sure knowledge that it was *not* the will of God that thousands die on September 11, that when the planes crashed into the towers of the World Trade Center and into the Pentagon and onto the field in Pennsylvania, God's heart was the first of all our hearts to break.

Let us turn now to "America, land that I love." Like all of you I love America, yet never would I say, "My country right or wrong." That's like saying, "My grandmother drunk or sober." As Americans, we have to remember that discussion, debate, and dissension are hallmarks of our democracy, and as Christians, we're called on to engage in a lover's quarrel—not a grudge fight, but a lover's quarrel with our country, a reflection of God's eternal lover's quarrel with the entire world.

We do rightly to distinguish individual persons from nations. When Kenneth Angell, Vermont's Roman Catholic bishop, told his parishioners that he must forgive the hijackers he was in no way implying that it would be easy; after all, his brother and sister-in-law were aboard American Airlines Flight 11, which crashed into the World Trade Center. Nor was the bishop softening the brutality of the hijackers' crime. It is precisely what cannot be condoned that can only be forgiven. Bishop Angell was simply saying that retribution was not the way of Jesus, a reminder that Christianity, far from being tried and found wanting, has been tried and found exceedingly difficult.

For a nation, as opposed to an individual, the highest moral ideal is generally not forgiveness but justice. Let me repeat: God hates hateful things, God hates injustice. In the Bible the first recorded murder is a fratricide, Cain kills Abel. "And the Lord said, 'What have you done? The voice of your brother's blood is crying to me from the ground.'" God is not mocked: The world swings on an ethical hinge; fuss with that hinge, and both history and nature will feel the shock. Life is consequential, criminals must be held accountable and punished if only by being left, like Cain, at the bar of history with a mark on his forehead. Nonviolence is not nonresistance to evil. Jesus, Gandhi, Martin Luther King, Jr., all resisted evil in very concrete ways.

That leads me to the bombing of Afghanistan, which began a week ago, October 7. We had suffered anguish. Gone forever were our sense of invulnerability and invincibility. Many people said, "September 11 changed the world." I never believed that. I believed it would be America's response that would change the world and just possibly for the better in far-reaching ways.

On September 20, the president said, "Whether we bring our enemies to justice or bring justice to our enemies, justice will be done." This eloquent sentence gave rise to the hope that justice might be rendered by law—by international law, by coalition building, by sharing intelligence, freezing assets, even by forceful extradition of terrorists if internationally sanctioned, and by trials before an international court.

The president didn't have to say that the terrorists declared war on America; he could have called them mass murderers, their deeds crimes against humanity in a legal technical sense. He could have added: "We will not respond in kind. We pledge not to kill innocent people. We will not seek to avenge the death of innocent Americans by the death of innocent victims elsewhere, lest we become what we abhor. We refuse to ratchet up the cycle of violence that brings only ever more funerals, destruction and deprivation, and ever more senseless rage." He might even have said, "Fellow Americans, we cannot ensure success, but we can deserve it."

But instead of embracing the force of law, he and the Congress embraced the law of force. Now we are dropping five-thousand-pound "bunker busters" and anti-personnel bombs that explode just before they hit the ground. Soon our troops will be on the ground. The number of innocent victims is growing.

So how shall we pray God to bless America, to "stand beside her and guide her through the night with the light" that does shine high over our own and every earthly flag?

The president has described the war as good versus evil, and at his Thursday night press conference, he expressed amazement that anybody should dislike America except out of envy. The trouble with so many Americans, including our leaders, is that we are too innocent to recognize our own lack of innocence.

Millions of Muslims dislike us for good reason. They deeply resent our troops' being stationed since the Gulf War in Saudi Arabia, home of the two holy sites of Mecca and Medina. Why, we have to ask, were they still there? Muslims also remember our misplaced retaliation against the Sudanese pharmaceutical enterprise and are convinced that we are highly partial to Israel at the expense of Palestinians, that our market economy allows the rich to hoard the best of the world while freezing poor people out, and that Americans are undermining the freedom of countless Arabs by supporting their corrupt and tyrannical governments. Although most Muslims did not support the hijackers, many considered their violence a predictable result of American foreign policy. Said one of them some time ago: "The warning sirens are wailing but who in Washington is listening?"

So God bless America with humility lest our pride-swollen faces close up our eyes. Said Augustine: "Never fight evil as if it were something that arose totally outside of yourself." In other words, love your enemy, in part because you made him so.

Violence is equally degrading, if not equally fatal, to those who use it and those who suffer from it. To quote Augustine again, "Imagine the vanity of thinking that your enemy can do you more harm than your enmity." Therefore may God help us to defuse our hatred, to make our worldly grief godly grief.

Of Afghanistan we have to ask: "What's left to ruin?" After twenty-three years of war and four years of fearful drought, her people live in pitiable conditions, four million as refugees, and many see themselves as the first victims of the oppressive Taliban. So I pray God to help us listen to the voices of suffering, to keep our hearts tender.

Were we in the near future to turn from the law of force to the force of law and view the struggle not as good versus evil, but as evil versus peace; if Americans today see the freedom that makes us vulnerable as the same freedom that is our great strength; if strangers continue to embrace one another on our streets, and if our country seriously embraces multilateralism, and the nations of the world come to care for twenty-six million Afghans, and thereafter the millions who suffer comparable poverty—then, like Jesus, we shall behold Satan "fall as lightning from the sky" (Lk. 10:18).

It's hard, of course, to be optimistic. Being close to power isn't the same as being close to reality. But let us remember how bleak was the scene, how dismal was the future to the eyes of Habakkuk, who still went on to say: "Yet I will rejoice in the LORD; I will exult in the God of my salvation." He understood that God's grace wends its redemptive way through the disorders of the world and that religious folk must keep the faith, despite the evidence, knowing that only in so doing has the evidence any chance of changing.

Look over at the altar, covered as it has been for weeks with symbols of hope. "Over all our wounded Mother Earth are flying not only terrorist planes; cranes still fly, too" (Yevgeny Yevtushenko). And never forget Vaclav Havel: "Hope is not the conviction that something will turn out well, but the certainty that something makes sense, regardless of how it turns out." What makes sense, eternal sense, is "God is love, and they who abide in love abide in God and God abides in them." With that understanding, may God bless America.

Hospitality

16

Opening to Community

Claudia Ann Highbaugh

My dear friend and colleague Harry Baker Adams was the house master of Trumbull College, one of the residences at Yale. Each college worked to have its own personality. The student and the house masters worked to make the college home away from home.

When Harry's predecessor at Trumbull College left the master's house, his gift to the college was thousands of daffodil bulbs. The bulbs waited for some time to be planted, until Harry, an early riser, decided to plant them to give the Trumbull College courtyard a beautiful coat of spring color. He invited some of the students from the college to join him in his early morning task. A few of the seniors joined in. Digging and planting, planning and plotting, they laid in the thousands of bulbs in the spring of 1989. Most of the associate gardeners would graduate and never know the lovely light of their springtime blessing![1]

---

[1] Harry B. Adams shared this story with the staff of the Yale chaplain's office when the flowers bloomed in the spring of 1999. I went to the courtyard to see the daffodils. That lovely yellow blanket is forever part of my memory.

The old chaplain's office at Yale was located in the freshman yard, in a one-hundred-year-old edifice that had once been the library. The building, now gutted for student organizations and the work of the university ministry, possessed two wings of offices and an old, gothic inner core that survived as one of the university chapels. Dwight Hall was home to one of the better university organs, the student volunteer organizations, and the staff who coordinated the campus chaplaincy and the ministry organizations. The organ was played for practice, fourteen to eighteen hours a day; the tiny little kitchen bustled with preparations for coffee breaks and small receptions; and the doors were constantly opening and closing with the comings and goings of students, faculty, community volunteers, alums, and on occasion the homeless. The old hall was bustling all day and into the night with the life of the university, the faith communities and even the town of New Haven.

I lived and worked in this place as associate university chaplain with the university chaplain, Harry B. Adams. In a small suite of offices, we planned worship, organized student life programs, coordinated the work of the campus ministries, and most important, held open a space of hospitality and welcome for our students all day long. The little office suite, overflowing with staff associates, staff assistants, and work/study students, was always equipped with soda, a fresh pot of coffee, cookies and the requisite M&M's, our office trademark. The door to the chaplain's office was open from nine in the morning until all hours of the evening. Students came in to chat, grieve, grow, study, and write papers. They came to find company and comfort, a home, safe space and time for listening, laughter. These were our tasks.

In the early Christian tradition, hospitality was the task of those living in communities to nourish and protect travelers. Hospitality was an act of welcome. Acts of hospitality were those demonstrations of generous reception that extended the welcome of a living unit or a family over the threshold and into the warm, safe, and nourishing safety of a residence or dwelling. Ancient hospitality provided a transition, a rest for the traveler. Once the invitation was extended to the traveler to come inside, an offering was made to them of refreshment and sustenance.

It is not too difficult to imagine welcoming the eighteen- to twenty-five-year-old stranger into the safety and security of our old chaplain's office suite. In the first months and years of school, whether they were entering as undergraduates or in the early days of a graduate degree, all the young people who crossed our threshold came loaded down with the usual baggage of books, clothing, stereos, and things to cook with in the dorm. In the later years, there were even giant boxes of computer stuff that some students had to learn to use. And they came with ideas and ideals and expectations of home and head and heart and family. Our little threshold was a way station set amidst the crisscrossed and worn paths of the centuries-old campus. We waited all day, every day to be an oasis.

Under the guidance and persuasive supervision of the Reverend Harry Baker Adams, our cast of associates, staff, and student workers began the long work day around mid-morning, 9:45 or so, with a pot of coffee, a refill of the M&M jar, an open box of chocolate chip cookies, and a stash of soda in the little fridge for the regular flow of visitors. It was impossible to think of the chaplain's office suite as a formal business operation. The business got done. Papers were filed, articles were written, bulletins and newsletters were regularly printed by their deadline. But the basic activity of the day, each day was to be ready to meet and greet and host the daily parade of personalities, seekers, friends, and colleagues. We were there to welcome those who would come to the doorway to ask for directions or seek counsel on a course or major. We waited out identity crises, watching the crises grow and the identities take shape. We laughed at jokes and bad lectures. We discussed the classics, politics, religion, sex and sexuality (of course), family relations, race, class, and body image. The curriculum of the office banter was at least as exciting as any major in the catalogue, and it was totally unpredictable.

The soda pop and cookies were the simple nourishment for the unending nurture provided in the little suite in the middle of the freshman yard at Yale.

The ancient idea of providing nourishment and sustenance for the traveler seeking comfort at a way station is a sound basis for the work of college chaplaincy. A good, stationary, dependable space for refreshment accommodates the students' journey with rest stops as needed. One of the most important things about a place of hospitality is that it needs to be a place that derives its nature, comfort, refreshment, and the gift of renewal from a reputation of being, on a constant basis, available, open, and ready for guests.

The old chaplain's office in Dwight Hall was situated in the campus center for volunteer service. Most students found time to give some energy, talent, and creativity to the community. Bustling with activity, Dwight Hall was one of the centers for student life and engagement at Yale. It was a place to be, and a place to find things to do. The constant music of the practice organ, daily prayers at 5:00 p.m., dozens upon dozens of posters for student organizations, events, and volunteer opportunities gave the building an ambiance of openness and possibility. A hospitable space needs to be in a place where people want to be.

An important aspect of college ministry is the opportunity to be a way station for daily passages, or even a kind of station with signals, signs, and directions that help a young person to find his or her way or just choose a short-term destination. Much like Grand Central Station in New York City, a space busy with people touching base, asking directions, looking for times and places, finding a good scone and the perfect cup of coffee, waiting with lots of other people from lots of other places; this is one good way to be a welcoming place for students. It is one good, satisfying model of ministry.

This kind of work demands a good amount of openness and not much judgment. There have to be some comfortable chairs, not too many clocks. There is a lot of time spent listening to what some would think is nonsense. The point is to be patient, so there is an opportunity to create good sense. Being a way station, equipped with a small variety of waiting tools, is a good way to make a contribution to the sustenance of individuals and the larger community.

In addition to the obvious constant supply of snacks, solid food on occasion works wonders! Dining hall food is a necessity. Providing opportunities for dining, in the student community, is a hospitable way of building and creating new relationships with meals, warm and homemade, the "stick to your ribs" kind that gets folks to sit together in an unusual configuration. This complement to nourishment will allow students to meet and eat and get to know one another, and have some good discussion on the questions that never seem to go away.

In the Common Room of Dwight Hall, we tried a few things to ignite community and personality over a good meal or a culinary treat.

Late at night over soda and chips, a gathering of more than a hundred students from backgrounds of different races began a conversation that explored the ways that they lived in common. Together, they rethought the teachings of a past generation that assumed one race's lives were different from others. The open space, where these young people were invited to talk about who they were and to examine their ideals, their cross-cultures and magnificent mixes of lives, survived for several terms as a study break group and evolved into a dinner group. Permission to work out differences over a hot plate of enchiladas created a sustaining bond.

One year for Black History Month, a colleague and I held a dessert event, "Sweet Memories and Sweet Potato Pie." My friend Frank and I cooked up a dozen pies and delivered them to the hall with a couple of gallons of milk. Students were invited to bring their favorite poem, story, song, or quotable wisdom from the African American tradition. The Common Room was packed. Students left behind their studies for a while. All left inspired and full of good humor.. There was a fine family kind of feeling. Milk and pie before bed can only enhance, engage, and stimulate the spirit of the people.

The end-of-the-semester study break is an age-old tradition for nourishment in times of stress. The chaplain's office was allowed to move to the Trumbull College residence to be a study aid for the hopeless and the hungry during reading period. If memory serves, the pizzas did not last long and the conversations did not linger. But the hot food, served up by the ministry staff as a break from the grind, was the perfect prescription for relaxation. Young adults have and need a great deal of energy to sustain their brain cells for all-nighters. The study breaks were encouragement and adult presence and support at the site of very difficult and stressful hours of study.

Although he may not remember or admit it, Harry B. kept a strict schedule for his own hospitable communication. Each day, promptly at 10:45, he would appear in the chaplain's office for one cookie and a cup of coffee. Chitchat and campus updates were the agenda. I learned to be present. I remembered to have the cookie at the ready. I sat with my question for the day, ready to listen to my mentor for a few minutes of reflection. This is when I learned from Harry Baker Adams that the biggest part of my job as associate was to be present, prepared, open, patient, and ready to receive the challenges and questions of the day. Our plan in the chaplain's office was not so much to structure the work of the day, but to attend to it. Working at all times to be alert to real crises, we spent days on end standing at the door, sitting in the big old leather chairs, listening, hearing, and delivering our cherished charges to the next step on their short passage through Yale.

At the end of the year, at the wonderful location of Dwight Hall, on the old campus where the commencement exercises were held, the big open door and several good cooks brought our graduates and their families to the Common Room for a farewell luncheon. The table was overflowing with food, the room with people, and the air was electrified with anticipation of the close of the journey. The ease and comfort of the small office suite, transported downstairs for the farewell supper, reminded our charges that all good company, all good food, and all good journeys are based on the right location, an open door, and the sharing of good memories.

In the summer of 1989, David Salzman, a resident in Trumbull College, was diagnosed with a terminal cancer. David, who had graduated earlier in the spring, had been one of the planters of the daffodils in the Trumbull College garden courtyard. In the early chilly hours of the new spring morning, with Harry B. and his classmates, David had planted a few hundred of the bright yellow daffodil bulbs. In the fall, David died. In the spring of 1990, the courtyard of Trumbull College came alive with thousands of bright yellow daffodils. David's parents visited there—and remembered.[2]

Just inside the gate, and across the threshold of the main Trumbull College entry, all are invited to come and sit and rest awhile. Enjoy the spring, the new light of the massive carpet of yellow flowers. Come and sit, rest awhile, and remember!

---

[2]This part of Harry's story about the garden is made in memory of David Salzman, Yale Class of 1989.

17

"The Dynamics of Honesty"

Stephen Butler Murray

This sermon was delivered at The Scarsdale Congregational Church in Scarsdale, New York, on January 27, 2002.

> You shall not have in your bag two kinds of weights, large and small. You shall not have in your house two kinds of measures, large and small. You shall have only a full and honest weight; you shall have only a full and honest measure, so that your days may be long in the land that the Lord your God is giving you. For all who do such things, all who act dishonestly, are abhorrent to the Lord your God. (Deut. 25:13–16)

When we hear this passage from Deuteronomy, there is an unmistakable value placed on the virtue of honesty. Unlike many passages in the Bible, the message is rather simple. Metaphorically using the weights and measures of business, the very tools of trade at the time of ancient Israel, the text tells us that we should not have one set of scales that undervalues and another set of scales that overvalues. Rather, we are instructed to have a "full and

119

honest measure," the sort of scale that reliably bears true. The result is that sometimes we may pay more than what we wanted to, and there are times that we may get less for what we brought to the table than we thought we would. Our financial well-being may suffer for it, but the very intrinsic value of honesty must be kept sacred in all our dealings.

While this passage deals specifically with issues of economic integrity, I think that it propels us toward thinking about the very dynamics of honesty on a larger level. As we live in the larger world, we constantly encounter situations in which we decide whether we shall be honest. There is not a day that goes by in which we do not teeter on the edge of speaking truths or falsehoods, sometimes in the most subtle and seemingly harmless of ways.

But I do not want to talk about honesty in a simple way, wagging my finger and saying, "We should all be good, upstanding citizens!" We all know that! What I want to talk about instead is the very underlying dynamics of honesty. About why, when we approach other people, our honesty is what shines forth time and again as the measure of our own integrity, of our respect for others and our own respectability.

I think that it begins with who we are on our own, with our own quest for authenticity. It is difficult to be honest with others if we cannot be honest with ourselves. When we look in the mirror at the end of the day, do we see someone that we have crafted or do we see ourselves? When we listen to ourselves talk, do we speak in a manner that sounds like us, or have we contrived our speech to how it would fit best in the situation? Are we able to face our weaknesses in such a way that we can laugh at ourselves, rather than grimace when others hone in on our flaws and point them out? Do we only play to our strengths, or do we allow ourselves the vulnerability of trying out new things that might instead explore the ways that we are inexperienced? These are all questions regarding how we view ourselves and whether we are able to have real integrity in our own self-assessments.

It seems to me that when we are able to regard ourselves accurately, when we truly know who we are, that we enjoy a certain freedom. We are free because we recognize the ways that we are lacking, rather than mythologizing our weaknesses into fatal flaws. We are free because we are not bound by our strengths into thinking that they are all that we have to offer. Being authentic with ourselves means that we are able to act broadly, courageously, daring ourselves to stretch beyond our limits and our limitations.

This is also true when we interact with each other. When we are honest with one another, we can move out of *relationships* of mere convenience and into *friendships* of deepening intimacy. What is stunning and beautiful is that in those times, as we grow into greater and greater intimacy, we establish, together, a freedom that neither of us could possibly enjoy on our own. That is because in friendship we enjoy a freedom that is interpersonal, a freedom that goes beyond our own accounting for who we are. In friendships, not only are we honest with ourselves but we also are honest with each other. It is expected and understood as the very basis of our bond together. Honesty is what makes relationships possible, for honesty is the very foundation of the respect, cooperation, and reliability that we feel toward one another when we really, truly are friends.

Of course, among the most beautiful of friendships are those that bloom into marriages. After my fiancée and I announced our engagement to our friends and family, we began receiving letters of congratulation. A letter that touched us greatly was written by Douglas Sturm, a professor from my undergraduate days at Bucknell University, whose classes on religious ethics were decisive in my decision to attend seminary. He is a Methodist minister whose pastoral tone has mixed with his professorial advice to me throughout the last nine years. Here is an excerpt from Doug's letter that I think says something of what a truly good friendship is meant to be:

> Let us indeed trust that you and she will find continuing inspiration in each other, that each of you will learn what it is to transform one's identity through the co-commitment of marriage, that together you may make an even more creative impress on the world than you could possibly accomplish singularly, and that those around you both will find joy in your new presence.

My former professor continues to teach me still. Friendship is never something that shapes and changes only the participants that have built the bond. Rather, friendship is something that is shared on a larger level, affecting others who come into contact with the friends and their collaborations. Together, in relationship, we become far greater than we were on our own. When we build honest, good friendships, we find our own character and mettle tested, challenged, and proved far more than it ever would have been, left to our own devices. By being together, the opportunities to become better than we were before arise constantly.

When we are hospitable, we do not commit the sin of utter self-reliance. To be hospitable is to believe that others can help us *and* we desire that others be of help to us. The way that we receive other people with a generous, compassionate spirit oftentimes is emblematic of how we receive God. If we cannot and will not receive others into our lives, chances are we also do not seek any sort of companionship with God. God may be there, at the borders of our vision and edges of our consciousness, and we may respect God's presence, but we do not yearn for God to be a vital part of who we are and what we do. It is one thing to realize that God exists, but another thing entirely to chance being transformed by a relationship with something so indefinable and mysterious as a God who loves us through all.

Last year, the BBC conducted a nationwide survey to determine what the people of Britain thought was the greatest book that had been written in the last century. And number one overall was not *a* book, but a trilogy, J.R.R. Tolkien's *The Lord of the Rings*. And I shall admit, since I first read the trilogy when I was about nine years old, it has been one of my favorites as well. Last month, I was chomping at the bit to see Peter Jackson's movie of the first book in the trilogy, *The Fellowship of the Ring*.

When I watched the film a couple days after Christmas, I remembered one of the reasons that I found the book so compelling, both as a child and as an adult: I believe that Tolkien had a good sense for the nature of evil. The true danger of the magical ring at the center of his tale is that it is utterly corruptive. No one exposed to it is immune to its siren call. And what is so insidious about its power is that the ring does not prey on the weaknesses of its wearer, but on the wearer's best, most noble traits, on one's virtues. It is the warrior Boromir's loyalty to his people that is corrupted, not his lack of hope. The wizard Gandalf fears that his compassion, his desire to do good, would merely be the instrument for the ring, through him, to accomplish great evil.

In effect, the ring undermines the true, authentic self of the wearer. Instead, it woos its bearer into believing that with the ring, the bearer can accomplish great things and wield unspeakable power. But in truth, the ring merely bends the character of the one who holds it toward callousness and malice. The bearer loses the ability to discern the world correctly, because he has lost all honesty about himself and others. Everyone is suspect, everything is a potential enemy. The mind cannot find rest, obsessed solely with keeping the precious ring.

I believe that is the nature of evil: It wrecks our ability to be honest with ourselves, and that does not happen only in realms of fantasy. It happens in our lives when we are overcome with uncertainty, when we lose hope. When life just simply gets too hard. Perhaps Psalm 40 says it best: "For evils have encompassed me without number; my iniquities have overtaken me, until I cannot see; they are more than the hairs of my head, and my heart fails me" (v. 12). In those moments, we either succumb to the trials and tribulations of life's meaner offerings, or we can turn in intimacy to the one with whom we can always find freedom, and that one is God.

Before, I said that it is in relationships defined by intimacy that we find who we are at our core, our most true and authentic self, that aspect of ourselves that nothing, *nothing*, can erode away. And in a certain way, the most intimate of relationships that we can establish is the one that we might have with God. And most often, the way that we share with God is in and through the activity of prayer. When we pray, we encounter God in utter honesty. There is no part of ourselves that we can veil or disguise or feign or adorn. God sees us for who we are, and so we enter into that relationship with God knowing that there can be nothing but truth therein. If we avail ourselves of anything but honesty in our communications with God, all that we do is fail to recognize that we are the only ones fooled. God knows us deeply and completely, and it is our prerogative to decide whether we will let that knowledge fill us with strength or cast us into worry.

You see, that is the beauty of prayer. We can simply let go. Prayer, when done right, is effortless. We do not need to send fancy words up to God. We do not need to armor ourselves in classical rhetoric or consult our internal speechwriters. God does not and cannot be swayed by our persuasive skills. The only preparation that we may need to go through, in order to pray well, is simply to release all of our expectations of what great speech is. All we need to do is be ourselves, however we are. If we are in the midst of a great success, then we can encounter God with a phenomenal grin on our face. If we find ourselves in a time of mourning and loss, then we can face God with tears streaming down our cheeks. All that matters is that we be honest with ourselves as we step into that time of oneness with God. For within that space of prayer, God will find us as we are, whether we intend it or not.

I, for one, find great comfort in the fact that my dearest friendships, my best relationships, my moments with God, require nothing false from me. I do not need to buck up. I do not need to put on a false front. I do not need to pretend to be stronger than I am, happier than I feel, wittier than I can muster. Those that know us well, those that love us not just when it is convenient, but when it is hard, do not require us to always show ourselves at our best. In fact, it would be a disappointment to them if we were to display a false persona, a fake measure of how we are. It is when we are in intimate relationship to one another that we can be passionately, unabashedly honest. It affects us in the way we love, in the way we act, in the way that we perceive and approach the world. When we are honest, we rarely treat others shabbily. If we believe that they will be honest in return, we always can move forward in trust.

One of the theologians whom I admire most is Miroslav Volf of Yale Divinity School. Volf is a Pentecostal Presbyterian from Croatia, and is so committed to his roots that every year he spends some months back in that war-torn country teaching at an evangelical seminary. He recently won the prestigious 2002 Grawemeyer Award in Religion for his book *Exclusion and Embrace*. Volf focuses on "what kind of selves we need to be in order to live in harmony with others." In addressing the topic, Volf stresses the social implications of divine self-giving. He says that the scriptures attest that God does not abandon the godless to their wrongdoing, but gives of God's self to bring them into communion. We are called to do likewise—"whoever our enemies and whoever we may be." The divine mandate to embrace as God has embraced is summarized in Paul's injunction to the Romans: "Welcome one another, therefore, just as Christ has welcomed you" (Rom. 15:7).

Obviously, Volf bears some high expectations for how we are to act in the face of adversity. I want to close the sermon this morning with a short story from the introduction of Volf's acclaimed book that I think displays some real honesty. In the winter of 1993, Miroslav Volf had finished giving a lecture when

Jürgen Moltmann, who had directed both of Volf's doctoral dissertations at the University of Tübingen, stood and asked, "But can you embrace a *cetnik*?" For months, the Serbian freedom fighters called *"cetnik"* had been sowing desolation in Croatia, herding people into concentration camps, burning down churches, and destroying cities. Volf had just argued that we ought to embrace our enemies as God has embraced us in Christ. So the question was could he embrace a *cetnik*, the ultimate other. For Volf, the evil other. What would justify the embrace? Where would he draw the strength for it? What would it do to his identity as a human being and as a Croat? It took a while for Volf to answer, though he immediately knew what he wanted to say. "No, I cannot—but as a follower of Christ I think I should be able to."

I *like* that answer. It seems to say that honesty does not require us to act in a superhuman way that betrays our loyalties and personal values. Rather, what honesty really calls us to do is come face to face with our God. Honesty is recognizing the ideal of what God would have us be, and what God would have us do, even if we cannot quite reach it. Amen.

18

"Matter Matters"

Barbara K. Lundblad

Then he brought me back to the entrance of the temple; there, water was flowing from below the threshold of the temple toward the east (for the temple faced east); and the water was flowing down from below the south end of the threshold of the temple, south of the altar. Then he brought me out by way of the north gate, and led me around on the outside to the outer gate that faces toward the east; and the water was coming out on the south side.

Going on eastward with a cord in his hand, the man measured one thousand cubits, and then led me through the water; and it was ankle-deep. Again he measured one thousand, and led me through the water; and it was knee-deep. Again he measured one thousand, and led me through the water; and it was up to the waist. Again he measured one thousand, and it was a river that I could not cross, for the water had risen; it was deep enough to swim in, a river that could not be crossed. He said to me, "Mortal, have you seen this?"

Then he led me back along the bank of the river. As I came back, I saw on the bank of the river a great many trees on the one side and on the other. He said to me, "This water flows toward the eastern region and goes down into the Arabah; and when it enters the sea, the sea of stagnant waters, the water will become fresh. Wherever the river goes, every living creature that swarms will live, and there will be very many fish, once these waters reach there. It will become fresh; and everything will live where the river goes. People will stand fishing beside the sea from En-gedi to En-eglaim; it will be a place for the spreading of nets; its fish will be of a great many kinds, like the fish of the Great Sea. But its swamps and marshes will not become fresh; they are to be left for salt. On the banks, on both sides of the river, there will grow all kinds of trees for food. Their leaves will not wither nor their fruit fail, but they will bear fresh fruit every month, because the water for them flows from the sanctuary. Their fruit will be for food, and their leaves for healing." (Ezek. 47: 1–12)

"There was a rich man who was dressed in purple and fine linen and who feasted sumptuously every day. And at his gate lay a poor man named Lazarus, covered with sores, who longed to satisfy his hunger with what fell from the rich man's table; even the dogs would come and lick his sores. The poor man died and was carried away by the angels to be with Abraham. The rich man also died and was buried. In Hades, where he was being tormented, he looked up and saw Abraham far away with Lazarus by his side. He called out, 'Father Abraham, have mercy on me, and send Lazarus to dip the tip of his finger in water and cool my tongue; for I am in agony in these flames.' But Abraham said, 'Child, remember that during your lifetime you received your good things, and Lazarus in like manner evil things; but now he is comforted here, and you are in agony. Besides all this, between you and us a great chasm has been fixed, so that those who might want to pass from here to you cannot do so, and no one can cross from there to us.' He said, 'Then, father, I beg you to send him to my father's house—for I have five brothers— that he may warn them, so that they will not also come into this place of torment.' Abraham replied, 'They have Moses and the prophets; they should listen to them.' He said, 'No, father Abraham; but if someone goes to them from the dead, they will repent.' He said to him, 'If they do not listen to Moses and the prophets, neither will they be convinced even if someone rises from the dead.'" (Lk. 16:19–31)

There's a new state park in Manhattan—Riverbank State Park—aptly named, for it sprawls along the banks of the Hudson River on the edge of Harlem. Yet, the park isn't exactly on the *banks* of the river...rather up *above* the river—but not on a hill. This new park is not really on the ground. Strange, but true. This park—complete with trees, ice skating rink, running track, concession stands, fields of grass, walkways—is not on the ground: It is on top of the sewage treatment plant. One of the largest public works projects in this country, the expansive gray building with a park on top, treats waste water on its way to the Hudson River. While kids skate, the water flows. Beneath the bikes and trikes of summer, the water flows. Under the slam dunks, under the park bench where lovers kiss, under the playground laughter—the water flows and the Hudson River begins to come back to life.

> "Wherever the river goes, every living creature that swarms will live, and there will be very many fish, once these waters reach there. It will become fresh; and everything will live where the river goes." (Ezek. 47: 9)

Wonderful words, Ezekiel...but you weren't thinking about the Hudson River water treatment facility, were you? The water in your vision is flowing from the temple, from the throne of God. The sacred river, the river shared by many cultures, the river later flowing in the visions of Revelation. "Shall we gather at the river, the beautiful, the beautiful river? Shall we gather at the river that flows by the throne of God?"

We can try, but it's hard to gather on the shore of a metaphor.

This river *is* a metaphor, isn't it? Purifying waters, cleansing the people of Judah. This vision comes from God—and from what you have seen, Ezekiel. Waters stagnant as the Dead Sea, the memory of an oasis in a barren place, rivers teeming with fish. But Ezekiel, you didn't expect us to take this picture literally. There is no river flowing under the temple door. (There isn't even a temple, let alone a temple door!) This is the stuff of visions: promises in the midst of mourning, hope springing up from despair. It's like your other vision—dry bones rattling to their feet, bone to bone, sinew to sinew, skeletons breathed back to life again. But not literally. And this vision, not literal either. God will purify and renew the people, not the river.

But what if Ezekiel's vision was larger than he could see—even with his ecstatic wisdom? Did God offer visions deeper than the prophets could fully understand? Is God waiting for others to fill them in? bring new meaning? Is there a river here after all? I have not come to psychoanalyze Ezekiel—but I am intrigued and delighted by his mention of the marshes: "But its swamps and marshes will not become fresh; they are to be left for salt" (Ezek. 47:11).

Could it be an early plea on behalf of the wetlands! Surely Ezekiel didn't know what Pastor Sharon Betcher knows—that wetlands "which include marshes, bogs, sloughs, floodplains and swamps, are the richest ecosystems on earth. Seventy-five percent of American bird species depend on roosting in wetlands; ninety percent of oceanic life begins in estuaries."[1] Don't mess with the marsh! Or is the marsh a metaphor?

A metaphor always points somewhere, moving us from the familiar to the strange, connecting words, images, or ideas to expand the way we see. Scripture is filled with metaphors from the created world—water flowing in the desert, flowers springing up in the wilderness, vineyards planted and ruined, mustard seeds and rising dough, a shoot growing from a stump clear-cut off. But usually we remove the metaphors too quickly from their earthly roots. Ezekiel's river isn't really a river. The metaphors go only one way—up, up, up to a spiritual world freed of matter. And they never come down to earth again.

Dr. Joseph Sittler, one of my mentors in the faith, spent a lifetime trying to bring us down to earth. He spoke the word *ecology* before it was in the newspapers or college catalogs; he connected the words *ecology* and *faith*. He wanted us not only to see the world but also to behold the world and be changed, saying, "With our minds we *look* at things, but in the spirit of our minds we *behold*

---

[1]Sharon Betcher, "An Ecofeminist Account of the Redemptive Value of 'Wet Lands'," *The Living Pulpit* 2, no. 2 (April-June, 1993): 23.

things…To behold a thing means to regard it in its particularity— its infinite preciousness, irreplaceability, and beauty."[2]

Dr. Sittler would ask us to behold the river. *Wade in the water, children!* For Sittler, theology was not a stagnant pool; it was always moving somewhere:

> By *theology* we mean not only a having but a doing—not only an accumulated tradition, but a present task which must be done on the playing field of each generation in actual life. One has a theology, to a greater or lesser extent, in order to do theology.[3]

Dr. Sittler invited pastors and professors and seminarians to engage new conversation partners to explore the metaphors of faith, to behold the physical world in all its precious fragility with the eyes of faith and eyes that see what we have failed to notice. *People will stand fishing from En-gedi to En-eglaim*—maybe even someday in the Hudson River! Can Ezekiel's vision move back to earth as well as away? A new conversation is desperately needed: Hebrew scholars and theologians, urban rangers and fishery experts, environmentalists and parish pastors, lovers of wetlands and seminary professors. All in the same circle.

Maybe, there's a river here after all. And if a river, maybe a table too.

Is Jesus' story of Lazarus and the rich man a metaphor? Is it a parable pointing to heavenly promises beyond earth's miseries? Are all those banquets in Luke metaphors for an abundant spiritual life? Or did Jesus really mean that the blind and the lame, the poor and the maimed would eat at the table? Is there any table here? Is there a rich man feasting sumptuously, never seeing—let alone beholding—Lazarus? Is Lazarus a metaphor?

In her book *The Body of God*, Sallie McFague urges us to see the table, and the people: "Jesus' eating stories and practices suggest that physical needs are basic and must be met—food is not a metaphor here but should be taken literally.[4] A bit later in the same chapter she insists: "The body of God must be fed."[5] In the church we have spent centuries focusing on the real presence

---

[2]Joseph Sittler, *Gravity and Grace* (Minneapolis: Augsburg Fortress Press, 1986), 16.
[3]Ibid., 65.
[4]Sallie McFague, *The Body of God: An Ecological Theology* (Minneapolis: Augsburg Fortress Press, 1993), 169.
[5]Ibid., 170.

of Christ at the communion table—but what about the real presence of food on the table for all of the world's people? Is that only a matter of politics—or is that, too, a matter of doing theology?

What sort of theology is McFague doing? No doubt there are more than a few theologians who are bothered by the central image of her book—the world as the body of God. It moves too close to pantheism for some. It is too bodily, too feminist, too Native American, too New Age. But what do we mean when we speak of "the body of Christ"? Is there any flesh on this metaphor? What happens when we begin to talk about the colors of this body? Can we fully see the body of Christ reflected in only one color? What happens when we struggle with what it means to move our churches toward greater diversity? Is this a theological commitment, a longing to be more fully the body of Christ—or is it solely, as some charge, a political agenda?

"Let's get back to the gospel!" we hear over and over, but what gospel is it that has no body?

The uproar over the Re-Imagining Conference in 1993 bears witness to our fear of bringing bodily metaphors down to earth (and into worship!). The angriest voices protested the language of the closing ritual, particularly the litany celebrating women's bodies. No doubt some who spoke and heard those words at the conference were embarrassed or at least surprised. (Dare I say it here? There were some who were also delighted, even ecstatic!) But those critics quoted most often in the press were disgusted and outraged, calling the liturgy pornographic, self-indulgent, hedonistic. Perhaps we wouldn't choose the same body-affirming litany for use in worship every Sunday. But in the years since that conference, I have asked myself, "When do we ever hear words that affirm the *body* in liturgy?" Do we ever thank and praise God for our physical, bodily selves? For arms that embrace, for muscle and bone? For our senses? For sexual pleasure? Is the body too disgusting? Can bodies only be metaphors in church?

Bodies matter to God. Matter matters. Until we can proclaim that wondrous reality, ecology will be a sidelight in our pastoring and preaching, our theologies and liturgies—as in the phrase, "Oh, I'm not into ecology." The gospel to which we return again and again is a Word *embodied*. The Word made flesh blesses this earth as holy ground—wetlands and rivers, wheat fields and dough rising, people dancing in the aisles and people sleeping in the streets of our cities. Matter matters to God.

Then he brought me back to the entrance of the temple; there, water was flowing from below the threshold (Ezek. 47:1a).

Water flowing down over the baptismal font, splashing the acolyte holding the worship book, soaking the carpet all the way to the front door—then out into the streets and on into Lake Michigan, soaking into the water table, flowing, flowing even as far as the Hudson River. Nearby, the children of Harlem play in the park on top of the water treatment plant. Later, it is hoped, they will run home to eat—food on the table and a roof over their heads. And Lazarus, who had been lying on the stoop, comes in to sit beside us at the table of God.

"Pass the bread, please," he says.

The body of Christ given for you, Lazarus.

He takes and he eats. And he knows it is more than a metaphor.

19

"Healing the Paralytic"

Claudia Ann Highbaugh

This was delivered as the 2000 Baccalaureate Sermon at Hiram College in Hiram, Ohio.

When he returned to Capernaum after some days, it was reported that he was at home. So many gathered around that there was no longer room for them, not even in front of the door; and he was speaking the word to them. Then some people came, bringing to him a paralyzed man, carried by four of them. And when they could not bring him to Jesus because of the crowd, they removed the roof above him; and after having dug through it, they let down the mat on which the paralytic lay. When Jesus saw their faith, he said to the paralytic, "Son, your sins are forgiven." Now some of the scribes were sitting there, questioning in their hearts, "Why does this fellow speak in this way? It is blasphemy! Who can forgive sins but God alone?" At once Jesus perceived in his spirit that they were discussing these questions among themselves; and he said to them, "Why do you raise such questions in your hearts? Which is easier, to say to the paralytic, 'Your sins are forgiven,' or to say, 'Stand up and take your mat and walk'? But so that you may know that the Son of Man has authority on earth to forgive sins"—he said to the paralytic—"I say to you, stand up, take your mat and go to your home." And he stood up, and immediately took the mat and went out before all of them; so that they were all amazed and glorified God, saying, "We have never seen anything like this!" (Mk. 2:1–12)

Greetings! The story that we have heard this morning is an unusual one. The Bible is filled with the miracles and healings of Jesus. We have heard many of them; they are familiar and comforting. The story upon story of miracle and healing are unbelievable and inspiring and even hopeful. When we hear and read them, we learn them. These stories become a text of our faith, but not part of the text of our lives. No one here feels that they can really perform a miracle. No one here feels that they can actually totally depend on miracles for recovery from illness. We have learned to rely on prayer and hope, but mostly we dote on the technical skills of the professionals, the vast resources of technology, and the possible discovery of a cure when we think of healing the sick.

This passage is interesting because it mixes the power of healing, which most of us do not have, with the power of possibility and determination, of making a way out of no way, which I would argue most of us do have!

And so here is my short lesson for you today. As you leave here today with brand new shiny tools, I am proposing that you use them to tear the roof off the impossible!

Let me try to reconfigure the story so that it will make more sense to you—in light of your new equipment, the resources that are yours as a result of your maturity, your experience, and this fine liberal arts education.

This is a story centering around a famous man who could work miracles, who told grand stories, and who was known in the community as a healer. Now a young man had some really amazing friends. The young man was suffering from a difficult and long-term paralysis, for which there seemed to be no cure. His friends cared deeply about him and were determined to help him move beyond his paralysis. They had heard that the great healer was in their community, so they determined that they would take the paralytic to him for the chance of a miracle healing. Actually, the friends knew that there was more than a chance of healing. They knew that if they could reach the healer, their friend would be cured of his paralysis. The friends of the young man determined that they would get him to the healer and that the healer would cooperate and make him walk again. As a matter of fact, the friends even convinced the paralytic that he should allow himself to be carried by four of them across town to the healer, so that he could be cured.

The friends came to the house where the healer was speaking to a crowd. They could not get into the house, for all access was blocked. They did not hesitate to follow through on their determined resolution for the paralysis. Having come to the place where the healer was residing to find the entry blocked and the crowd formidable, they moved to the roof!

In those days, the roof of a house was made of natural material, straw of some sort, mud…it was packed on, molded and messy. I guess that removal of such a domain cover required determined vigor. One would have to dig and pull and sweep to remove the roof of the house. The result would be that dust and dirt and mess would be stirred up everywhere. There is likely no way to be unobtrusive in such a determined endeavor. In moving the roof to lower an invalid, the team of determined friends must have made a huge, ugly mess. They had to pull and scrape and tug, covering themselves with dirt and dust, in order to create an opening large enough to lower their friend down into the house and to the source of healing.

Picture it, digging and pulling and tugging, to get the roof off of a house, so that you can bring your friend to life. I have no earthly idea what tools were available or even appropriate for such a challenging task. I cannot imagine how these friends would conceive of such an idea. But the text says here, with little detail, that "there was not room for them to gain access, not even in front of the door;" so the friends removed the roof.

This is my word for you today! *Tear* the roof off! You know, each of you what it is you are determined to do! Make a way, find an explanation, determine a route, a solution…tear the roof off!

The things you have that the friends of the paralytic did not have are shiny, brand-new tools for roof and barrier removal. Each of you is equipped with skills, resources, ideas, and finely tuned instruments for making progress, making a way out of what might to some seem impossible, tearing off the roof.

I like how this roof removal happens in the Bible story, and I appreciate very much the reason why it was necessary to remove the roof. There was no other way in! The friends determined that the only solution for the health of the paralytic was to create a way. They had to use their minds to come up with a solution for creating entry past the barriers, but the story is so matter of fact that we can only imagine how they got the roof off. They had to use their hands and the full strength of their bodies. They had to pull and tug and dig until there was a space, and a place big enough to enter the invalid into the house to receive the healer's blessing.

You're all better off than this biblical group of friends. You have, I am sure, become accustomed to varieties of difficult passageways and barriers. I am sure that many of you have ignored them, gone around them, over them, maybe even knocked down a few. But I am here to remind you this morning that equipped as you are, with a full tool belt, you are warned and reminded that there are those in our midst who are paralyzed. They need, require, and expect your help, your resources, your commitment. You have in your minds today solutions. You have in your hearts will, and you have as a result of your education, tools. Use them, now, to tear the roof off!

I know some people who do this roof removal thing for a living. I'll give you a few examples so that when you leave this place, you can get right at it!

Perhaps you have heard of Marian Wright Edelman. She is the head of an organization called the Children's Defense Fund. She thinks that a lot of the children in our culture, in this country, the United States of America, are paralyzed. Marian sees them unable to move and grow because they do not all have adequate housing and health care. Some of the children in the United States of America are struggling to learn because on a day-to-day basis, they do not have adequate nutrition, simply not enough to eat. Marian reminds us of the plagues of violence in our culture, teen pregnancy, inadequate parenting and formal family support systems. She invites all of us to join her in making a way out of no way, finding new ways to access possibilities for health, nutrition, and basic community support for our children. Marian Wright Edelman is screaming from the roof for all of us to join her in digging through the mess of inaccessibility. She is calling us to bring our tools to make a hole and to narrow the gap for our poor children. She suggests that we feel entitled to nothing and remember that tearing off the roof means that there will be some sweat and struggle.

Marian tells us to be confident, that even if some of us have smaller tools, or leaner resources, never forget that your work and determination will make a difference. Remember, she says, that before you, there were forebears on whose shoulders we stand. As we determine our new passageways, we must remember our roots, our history, and the heritage that is legacy for each of us.

Tools for clearing a way have to be sharpened. Don't ever stop learning and improving your mind. Your mind is your most important tool. And never, ever give up![1]

Some days, Marian Wright Edelman is up there all by herself, tools in hand, ripping away at the barriers to health and wholeness and healing for all of our children. But every day that I live and breathe, I can hear her voice speaking to me: Keep on pulling and tugging and clearing away the mess. Don't give up!

Maybe you know of my friend, Jonathan Kozol. He is a prolific writer. He writes about children and especially about the failure of our educational system to give each child proper tools. His first book, *Death at an Early Age,* was published in 1968, my freshman year at Hiram College. He has never stopped calling us to the roof! He thinks that all children deserve a strong educational foundation for life. He does not think that poor children should have used books, no heat in their school buildings, and day after day of inattention, simply because they have not had enough to eat.

Jonathan carries in his heart, every day, the spirit of paralyzed children. He thinks that all of us have to be their friends and go deep into the structure, even way below the roof, to heal the paralysis of children in the poorest schools in the United States of America. He will not allow us to forget that the tools we have earned are required for the destruction of "houses" of education: schools in poor communities that by their very presence become the structures of paralysis.

---

[1]Marian Wright Edelman, *The Measure of Our Success* (Boston: Beacon Press, 1992).

He tells us about a school in the South Bronx so poor that classes take place in settings like stair-landings, bathrooms, and coat closets, because the population of poor children is increasing but there are not funds to build schools for them.

He reminds me of my own roots and educational community. In suburban Chicago, at New Trier High School, one of the best in the country, every high school freshman is assigned a faculty adviser who counsels about two dozen students. At DuSable, in the inner city neighborhood were I grew up, each guidance counselor advises 420 students.

Not only does Mr. Kozol invite us to tear the roof off for the healing of the paralyzed. He also prods us to bring our tools and resources, our hearts and minds and intellect to the tasks of restructure, so that the new domiciles of education, by their very structure, defy lack of access, crowding, and paralysis.[2]

Perhaps these friends of the paralyzed seem vague and distant to you. But there is another I will name. In my years here as a college student in the late sixties and early seventies, the United States of America was in turmoil. The murders at Kent State and Jackson State happened thirty years ago, in my sophomore year. There were anti war demonstrations and even Klan presence in the dorms right here at Hiram College. The fear, anxiety, anger, and paralysis could have been our demise as an educational institution.

I remember being afraid for my life and my future. I remember feeling immobilized in a time when students were working to mobilize for change. Those were the years of the peace, affirmative action, and civil rights movements. I could not be mobilized by the anger and confrontation of my peers. I was afraid!

In the midst of these disturbing times, I took a class in which one young professor taught me to think for myself, to understand my presence and my gifts and my tools and my intellect as part of my history and my identity. He taught me to revere my past and to live, heads up and proudly, into the power and motivation of my own passion. This was my turning point. This is when I knew that my tool bag for access and entry for those in need of assistance would be the keys to a sound, relevant, and resourceful education. This is my passion and my inspiration, the man who tore the roof

---

[2]Jonathan Kozol, *Amazing Grace: The Lives of Children and the Conscience of a Nation* (New York: Crown, 1995).

off of my experienced limitations: David Anderson, a professor here in the English department at Hiram.

Mine is a task of education and the call to create and sustain systems of access for all of our children. This is at the heart of my life and work and ministry. It is in my daily prayers. And I, like you, stand on a firm educational foundation, nurtured, affirmed, and encouraged by the intentions of my teachers and mentors. I am here today because my very best teacher and most important mentor, David Anderson, taught me to reach into my deepest self, to know the strength of my passion. He taught me to live and work and believe in that passion. I work for justice. I live for truth. I am passionate about the education and quality of life for all of our children; for these things, I keep tugging away at the roof of structures of paralysis. My work is education. My job is to educate. My vocation is preaching truth to those in power.

You are the educated, the powerful, the friends of the paralyzed with the task of making a way out of no way. I challenge you to leave here today with an open mind and a sharp vision. Clear a path and make a way. Standing on the shoulders of my forebears: my family and the pioneers of the Christian Church (Disciples of Christ) who founded this college 150 years ago, I invite you to the world of work to serve, equipped with the tools of your own vocation and the determination to make a way, and new ways. I cannot leave without reminding you to keep your head and mind and vision pointed toward your passion.

On this great morning, you are invited to the roof! Climb up with me. Bring your tools, your creativity, your technical and analytical skills, your teaching abilities, your physical and emotional determination, your dexterity, your youth and vigor and verve! Let's get to work! Let's pull and push, and build and recreate. Let's all together make a way out of no way!

And hear these words of inspiration fromMaya Angelou:

Lift up your eyes
Upon this day breaking for you.
Give birth again
To the dream.
Women, children, men,
Take it into the palms of your hands,
Mold it into the shape of your most
Private need. Sculpt it into

The image of your most public self...
The horizon leans forward,
Offering you space
To place new steps of change
Here on the pulse of this fine day...
You may have the grace to look up and out
And into your sister's eyes,
And into your brother's face,
Your country,
And say simply
Very simply
With hope—
Good morning.[3]

And from the book of Philippians:

Finally, beloved, whatever is true, whatever is honorable, whatever is just, whatever is pure, whatever is pleasing, whatever is commendable, if there is any excellence and if there is anything worthy of praise, think about these things. Keep on doing the things that you have learned and received and heard and seen...and the God of peace will be with you.[4]

AMEN.
Women and men of the Class of 2000, tear the roof off the house!

---

[3]Maya Angelou, "On the Pulse of Morning," in *On the Pulse of Morning* (New York: Random House, 1993).
[4]Philippians 4:8–9.

20

"Pies on the Counter"

Carla Aday

This sermon was delivered on July 26, 1998, at Country Club Christian Church in Kansas City, Missouri.

> Now as they went on their way, he entered a certain village, where a woman named Martha welcomed him into her home. She had a sister named Mary, who sat at the Lord's feet and listened to what he was saying. But Martha was distracted by her many tasks; so she came to him and asked, "Lord, do you not care that my sister has left me to do all the work by myself? Tell her then to help me." But the Lord answered her, "Martha, Martha, you are worried and distracted by many things; there is need of only one thing. Mary has chosen the better part, which will not be taken away from her." (Lk. 10:38–42)

Granny never had a telephone. Oh, every now and then one of her twelve children would get frustrated and absolutely insist that a phone be installed in her home. But within a month or so, she'd have it unplugged or disconnected so eventually her children gave up. When we went to visit Granny, we always arrived unannounced. We'd just jump in the car after church on Sunday and drive down to her house in Frost, Texas, population 375. We'd try to make it before she got in her red pickup and headed out for the farm—without a driver's license, I might add. The thing that always amazed me about our visits to see my granny is that when we arrived—there would be two freshly baked pies on the counter—usually a lemon meringue and a coconut cream. "How did you know we were coming?" I queried my granny. "Oh, I didn't," and she would laugh. "I just thought some of my kids might come by today." Most of Granny's kids and grandkids lived fifty miles or more away, but she would take a chance that one of the twelve would show up, perhaps with grandkids in tow, to enjoy a Sunday afternoon treat. (And of course there was also an oversized cast iron skillet on the stove, with melted bacon grease in it, just waiting to fry up something for supper to go with those pies.)

My mother is my granny's daughter and I am my mother's daughter. We are heirs of something called southern hospitality. We know that you're supposed to fret a lot in order to feed a crowd. We know how to hover around the guests to make sure that their plates never go empty. We know that the hostess is expected to serve her guests an elaborate and piping hot entrée while staying engrossed in the stimulating dinner conversation and keeping the kitchen counters spotless. In fact, we may be direct descendants of a woman in the Bible named Martha, who also lived in the Southern Kingdom, in a little town called Bethany, near Jerusalem. Today's scripture lesson tells us that Martha went to great lengths to prepare a fancy supper for an extraordinary visitor passing through her town. The visitor's name was Jesus.

In preparing the feast for Jesus, Martha falls into a sacred tradition of hospitality whereby people welcomed the presence of God into their midst by serving food to one another. Abraham and Sarah prepare a dinner party for strangers in the desert who turn out to be messengers of God. God sustains the disillusioned followers of Moses with quail and manna, which gives them the courage to keep seeking the promises of God. The prophet Amos describes the good gifts of God as a fruit basket. Jesus turns water into wine at the wedding feast of Cana in Galilee, multiplies the loaves and fishes on the hillside in order to feed the masses, and sits at the supper table with his friends and lifts up the common elements of bread and wine to symbolize the new covenant of love between God and God's people.

Food takes on a sacred quality, not just in the Bible, but in our own lives as well. At our house, growing up, and even now when we all go home, we know again how much Mom loves us when we see her standing over the electric skillet frying chicken with one hand and stirring homemade banana pudding with the other. On mission trips in Venezuela, I have seen members from our church choke down one more *arepa,* a doughy tortilla usually cooked in burned grease, not because they liked the taste, nor even because they were hungry, but because eating the food offered by our hosts was a way of becoming partners in Christ. When a revered woman in this church died one day, another member told me that she remembered the soup that this woman had brought to her home some twenty years prior, during a time of grief. Feeding another is a holy thing. That's why today's scripture lesson puzzles me.

While Martha slaves away in the kitchen to fix Jesus and company dinner, Mary sits at the feet of Jesus, listening to his every word. Martha was distracted by her many tasks; so she came to Jesus and asked, "Lord, do you not care that my sister has left me to do all the work by myself? Tell her then to help me." But the Lord answered her, "Martha, Martha, you are worried and distracted by many things; there is need of only one thing. Mary has chosen the better part, which will not be taken away from her." You would think that Jesus could have at least called for "a round of applause for the ladies (or the one lady, as the case may be) in the kitchen."

Granny was no theologian. She spent far more hours standing over a cast iron skillet frying something in bacon grease than she ever did in church, but I think she would have a question or two for Jesus had she been present at the home of Mary and Martha. And there is enough of Granny in me to raise a few questions myself. Granny was practical. I remember one time when her daughter, my aunt, was in Europe for three weeks and Granny said to me, "I don't know why she would want to go over there. She's never going to live there." As the mother of twelve, and as a widow who ran the farm alone for thirty years after her husband's death, she was a busy lady. She must have canned a million jars of pickles in her lifetime. (But like all of us, Granny could be inconsistent, and blind to her own inconsistencies. She was a teetotaler, and her strong disdain for alcohol was fueled by two of her sons who had problems with drinking. But come Christmastime, Granny would sit by the fire for hours, drinking homemade eggnog that had more bourbon than whipping cream in it.) There is enough of Granny's no-nonsense approach to life in me to question Jesus a little about his motives and behavior at the home of Mary and Martha. I'd be tempted to ask Jesus, "Why scold the one doing the good works? Why take the side of Mary who sits around and leaves all the work to her sister?"

When I first studied this story about Mary and Martha, I thought Jesus was trying to say that the one thing we all really needed to do was to sit down and listen. "One thing is needful. Mary has chosen the better part." This didn't really make sense to me because in the story of the good Samaritan, which immediately precedes this story, Jesus had pointed to the good deeds of the Samaritan and said, "Go and do." So why this message: Sit and listen? Isn't the Christian life about doing good not just sitting around thinking about good things? Doesn't Jesus look at us when we become complacent and lazy, and call us to get up and get moving in the name of God? Doesn't Jesus call us to clothe the naked and feed the hungry? To serve on boards and teach Sunday school, to listen to a friend in need and write a check for a good cause?

Well maybe, just maybe, I mused, Jesus knows that when we do all that serving we sometimes become overburdened, cast down, worn to a frazzle, even burned out. Maybe in the midst of our exhaustion, God calls us to slow down and find the quiet center, to turn off the ringer, to go on a silent retreat, to stop by the chapel for silent prayer, to join a small group Bible study, to write in a journal, to seek spiritual guidance, to go to worship, to read a good book, to go to the symphony. Maybe the "one thing" that the Samaritan needed was to go and do, while the one thing Mary needed was to sit and listen. Maybe in order to fulfill that greatest of all commandments—to love God and love neighbor as self — we need times of activity and times of inactivity.

But Jesus said, "Mary has chosen the better part." What did he mean by that? Is he saying that it is better to lead a contemplative life of a monk than an active life as a Peace Corps volunteer? My granny would never buy that. In an article by David

Bartlett, preaching professor at Yale Divinity School, I was reminded that the problem with Martha is not that she was busy with great activity. The problem that Jesus called to Martha's attention is that she was distracted and anxious. Last week I was hurriedly preparing supper for my two-and-a-half-year-old son as he sat on the sofa drinking juice and eating crackers. "Mommy," he pleaded, "will you please come sit down and visit with me?" *We* easily become distracted and anxious. We worry about making it to all the kids' soccer games and saving enough for college tuition and being able to afford a family vacation...but do we hear what our kids say to us over the dinner table? We are afraid that the business will fail or that we will get passed over for promotion and in the midst of such pressing concerns, we lose sight of the job we are called to do. We come to church to hear the still, small voice of God, but our minds wander in a thousand different directions with our own worries. Even before telephones and car phones, speed dial and fax, even before voice mail and e-mail, Martha was just downright distracted with what was simmering on the stove. So distracted in serving Jesus supper that she couldn't even enjoy getting supper ready for Jesus.

Anne Neufeld Rupp, one of the speakers at Bible school this past week, shared with a group of parents about the night her teenage son returned home from camp. He was so eager to tell everyone about the fabulous experience he'd had at camp. He went out with his friends and then returned home at 11:30 p.m., sought out his mom and began talking to her about camp. She was exhausted, but still up doing laundry because the family was to leave at 3 a.m. for a family vacation. She just wanted to get the laundry done. But God intervened, she explained, and she sat down and listened to her son talk. Every parent of a teenager longs for those moments when your son or daughter will actually sit down and share what is on his or her heart. Here was just such a moment. Fortunately, she didn't get so distracted with the laundry task that she missed it.

It makes sense that Jesus would call for a balance of activity and inactivity and would caution us against becoming so distracted that we missed the joy of each day, but I still didn't understand why Jesus would say, "Mary has chosen the better part." Why side with Mary? It is important to note that Jesus doesn't bring this whole dispute up. Martha does. If Martha had not come to Jesus to complain that Mary was sitting on her duff, then Jesus would have minded his good manners as a guest and kept his mouth shut. But when Martha starts fuming in the kitchen about how mistreated she's been by her lazy sister, she draws Jesus into the sibling rivalry. Psychologists call this triangling, bringing in a third party. Rather than going to Mary and asking for a little help setting the table, Martha blames Mary for the predicament and asks Jesus to help fix it. All of us have our "Martha days," those days when we feel that all of the work has fallen to us and there is no one to help us with it. In times of stress like this, it is easy to find someone to blame, oftentimes someone close to us—a co-worker, a brother, a husband.

Blame attempts to find the source of the problem in one person and to preserve the goodness of the other. With blame no one wins. The best you can hope for is that the one who is blamed accepts the blame, and then feels ashamed. And that the one blaming feels justification for her anger. The result is that both you and the one you're blaming feel devalued and the gulf in the relationship is deeper and wider. So rather than helping Martha find Mary to be the guilty party, the one to be blamed, Jesus holds a mirror up to Martha, to help her see her own behavior. "Look how anxious you are, Martha. Perhaps that is why you are so frustrated." And he lets her off the hook and invites her to relax. The genius of Jesus is that he admonishes neither Mary nor Martha but frees each of them from what is binding them. Martha is freed from her worries and Mary is freed from the cultural restrictions of her day.

At the time of Jesus, it was neither customary nor proper for a rabbi to make a house call to a single woman. And yet sitting here in Martha's living room, Jesus breaks another cultural barrier by affirming the right of Mary to sit at his feet. The phrase "sit at the feet of" refers to becoming a student or disciple. The apostle Paul describes his own Jewish education by saying he was brought up "at the feet of Gamaliel" (Acts 22:3). Rather than stir the lamb stew, Mary decides to sit at the feet of Jesus and listen to him unlock the mysteries of the scripture, to reveal the truth about God. By upholding Mary's decision, Jesus makes a bold, radical move. He invites women to take their full and equal place alongside men who wish to follow God.

Long before women earned the right to vote, long before the Enlightenment, long before women's lib, long before scientists understood the biology of male and female, long before the

Southern Baptist Convention debated the role of women in marriage and ministry, and long before the pope banned women from the priesthood, Jesus liberated Mary and all women by inviting them to become disciples—full and equal partners of God in Christ. Jesus affirmed that a woman's place is any place God calls her to be—whether serving in the kitchen or translating Hebrew scriptures; she is fully a child of God.

The message Jesus taught to the disciples who gathered at his feet was: The lowly will be lifted up, the dead will be raised, the homeless will be given a home, the blind will see. By encouraging Mary to sit and listen rather than only scurry around in the kitchen, Jesus lifts her up. He models his own message. He lifts up the oppressed of his day and gives them new freedom and new life. The realm of God is now.

Much as I believe these messages from God come through this story loud and true, I think that to stop here would still miss the larger point of the event that takes place in Martha's home. "One thing is needful," Jesus replies to Martha. I think the "one thing needful" Jesus referred to was the feast of life he places before us—a life richer and deeper than what we often grow accustomed to. Martha was cooking up supper, but Jesus was preparing a feast from heaven, an opportunity to commune with God. Jesus is not all that concerned about whether we volunteer at the soup kitchen or sit and read the Bible. He just wants us to build our lives around the living God. Jesus calls the Marthas among us, who scurry around with our organizers scribbled full of "to do" lists, to keep our lives focused on God. And Jesus calls the Marys among us to find in our moments of solitude and reading and prayer the life-giving presence of Christ.

What truly nourishes us is the word of God, but we hunger for that which does not satisfy. We spend our days buying more clothes, building bigger houses, accumulating more stuff for our houses, earning more for our retirement accounts. We dine at the finest restaurants, drive through fast-food joints on every corner, and sip Starbucks gourmet coffee, but we still go to bed hungry at night. Jesus summons us to choose the better part, to build our lives around the one thing that makes all the other things meaningful. The "one thing needful," insists theologian Martin Niemöller, is Jesus himself. He offers us the nourishing gift of God's living presence. He gives the gift that cannot be taken away from us. He offers us life, a way of living so magnificent that it is eternal. He invites us to take off our kitchen aprons and sit down as guests at the table of God.

When I was a child and we would arrive at Granny's, I always had this little tinge of sadness when I saw those pies on the counter. "What if we hadn't come?" I wondered. What if we'd stayed for the church supper, or gone to the neighborhood picnic? What if I'd gone swimming with my friend, or stayed home to get my homework done? What if we hadn't come? What if none of the other children or grandchildren came either? Who would have eaten those pies?

Sometimes I imagine God's grace like that. As pies sitting on the counter. Just waiting for us to come by and enjoy the feast.